The Death and Resurrection of
Uncle George

To my
Uncle
From - Lieto
†Leonardo

LEONARDO HUTCHINSON

Cover Photo by chezbeate via www.pixabay.com under CC0 Creative Commons licence
Cover and Interior Design by Woven Red Author Services, www.WovenRed.ca

The Death and Resurrection of Uncle George/Leonardo Hutchinson—1st edition
ISBN ebook: 978-1-9995677-1-2
ISBN print book: 978-1-9995677-0-5

To Mom, who shares my belief that not everything is possible.

To Uncle who chased me around the soccer fields.
I turned out to be okay playing the wonderful game.

Table of Contents

The Hospital—Friday Night

As the Olympic Airways airplane was landing in Athens I woke up my mother. She opened her red and puffy eyes. They scanned my face.

"Leonarthe. Are we here?" she asked.

"Yes!" I answered. "Just a few more minutes for the plane to reach the terminal and we are here."

At 76 years old, the ten-hour trip from Vancouver, British Columbia to Athens through Frankfurt left its mark on her face. Mind you, I did not look any better. We had had hardly any sleep for the past two days as we left Canada for Greece with the shortest notice possible.

"It was a good trip. Don't you think?" she remarked.

"Yes. It was a good trip *Mana (Mom)*. As soon as we will get inside the airport, we need to rent a car and then we are off to Patra. Do we need to call Auntie Helen or do you think you know where we are going?"

"She told me where to go when she called me in Vancouver. There is only one hospital in Patra. She said we cannot miss it."

"Did she give you the address? Patra is not a small town, *Mana*!"

"Don't worry. We will find it. In the worst-case scenario, we will ask someone."

I decided not to say anything else about the point I was trying to make. It was almost five o'clock in the afternoon and if all went well, we would be reaching Patra close to 10 p.m. I was afraid that asking a Greek for directions late at night would guarantee us not to get to our destination.

"Do you want me to ask for a wheelchair, *Mana*? Or you're okay to walk?"

"I will walk. As long as you do not run ahead! I need to stretch my legs. Just get our stuff from the compartment. My purse is there."

"Yes. Don't worry. We are going to leave the plane last anyway."

I was not trying to be sarcastic. That was the way Mom travelled. She would board the plane first as a senior, but she would leave the plane last taking her time. In Frankfurt, she chose to ride the little airport go-cart. That ensured us that we would be on time to get the transfer plane to Athens.

"How is the weather? What time is it?"

"It is about 5 p.m. Athens time *Mana*. The weather is okay. There are just a few clouds in the sky; the sun is shiny enough for November. I thought it would have been raining this time of the year but I guess we are lucky."

"Yes. Raining starts in November," Mom murmured as she unbuckled her seat belt, following the directions provided by the plane's little signs over our seats. She reached down to grab her hat that was on the floor by the side of her chair. She calmly put it on her head and fixed her hair underneath it. She looked outside through the window as the plane was coming to a stop by the terminal.

"Yiorgo…," she sighed.

It took us about one hour to get our luggage, rent a medium-size Honda car for 30 Euros per day from Budget Rent-A-Car, and we were on our way toward Patra. The highway was busy this time on a Friday afternoon but nothing that I could not handle. After all, this was not my first time driving in Athens.

Last time I was in Greece, it was in July and August of 2007. I visited my relatives with my older son, Felitche. He was eleven at the time and I was forty-seven. Now, two years later, it was like déjà vu. The plane attacking the airport runaway coming from over the Aegean sea with Athens begging for mercy; the Parthenon still reaching high in distance; the passengers trying to leave the plane as fast as they could; the airport officer stamping the passports without looking at people's faces; the traffic relentless.

Mom was fully prepared for the tollbooths along the highway. She had quite a few Euros with her. When I asked her how she remembered to get some money for the tollbooths she was proud to announce that she still had her senses. In fact, she also came prepared with two maps—the map of Greece and the map of Peloponnese, just in case I could not find my way around.

"We are approaching Corinthos," I interrupted her.

She was talking about something but I was not paying attention. My mind was preoccupied trying to put everything into perspective. Mom calling me at work telling me that Uncle George had a major stroke; the trip arrangements; the fight with my wife, for she did not like the idea of me coming to Greece alone to "see my old girlfriends" as she put it. Life feels so uneven when something goes wrong and we have to change our routines and habits in a snap of two fingers.

"Yes!" she repeated. "Yes... do you want the map?"

"No. Do you want to stop and eat something? Are you

hungry?"

"No, I do not want to stop. We need to reach the hospital as soon as possible. I am not hungry. If you want, you can stop."

I smiled. That pretty much meant that we needed to keep going and our stomachs could suffer.

"Okay, *Mana*. Please pay attention to the road signs. I do not want to miss Patra's exit. If we both pay attention we cannot miss it."

"Good luck if you expect me to read the signs with how fast you are driving. And it is getting darker."

I sensed some frustration in her words but I was not about to ring any emergency bells. After all, the exit to Patra was coming up. I mentioned this to Mom and I noticed she relaxed in her seat.

They were fixing the road to Patra. Every 10 to 20 kilometers I had to reduce my speed and obey the signs indicating single lane with, "Workers working ahead for the next 5 Km". But we did not see anyone working all the way to Patra. And every other driver seemed to be irritated with me slowing down. A few passed me using the opposite traffic lane. Mom's answer to my observations was simple enough!

"No one works in Greece at this time of the night except in the clubs and the cafeterias."

It started to drizzle. I took a look at the car's clock: it flashed 9:25 p.m. Patra's outskirts were not adequately lit and the dark settled very quickly. I put on the wipers and the air to defrost the windows. I was not familiar with this type of Honda vehicle. A simple five-seat car designed not to use too much gas, automatic, and with air conditioning. I was very persistent with the Budget sales person in the airport that automatic with air conditioning and good gas usage were the most important features I was looking for in a car.

And it was almost new— 4,000 kms was the read of the odometer.

"*Mana*, we are inside Patra. Any ideas where the hospital may be located?"

"Auntie Eleni said we will see it from the highway. It is the biggest building."

"Yes, but it is dark and it is drizzling…and I cannot drive and look at the same time for the biggest building. Thank goodness there is no traffic now. I am going to turn in the next intersection and ask someone for directions."

That I did. A man was operating the little kiosk in the corner of the street. His head bent over the little window to take a look at me getting out of the car. He gave me directions to find the hospital and a little bit of a lesson.

"The construction of the hospital was completed in 1988 and it is the largest in the region of Peloponnese," he said proudly. "It has 800 beds you know, and it is affiliated with the University of Patras' School of Medicine. Many students come here to my kiosk to buy newspapers. In 2009, they changed the name you know, now it is called General University Hospital of Patras – All Holy Theotokos the Helper."

I turned around to get into the car that was still running before he finished his last sentence. I was rude, he probably thought, but as far as I was concerned time was of an essence. Nevertheless, his last words were projected and loud enough for me to hear.

The hospital was not far from the intersection where I turned. I drove back to the highway following the road signs leading to Athens, as we had already passed the "biggest building" in Patra. A few minutes later, I was entering the main hospital gates.

"You see, it was easy!" Mom proclaimed with excitement.

"And it stopped raining."

"Sure. It was not that I did not know big buildings; it was just that I had no means of comparing the biggest buildings in Patra."

"Just park! We need to hurry! I have to see my brother."

I screeched the tires of the car into the first empty spot I could find, bringing it to a raging halt. I rushed to the passenger side to help my mother. I held her hand as she groaned, struggling to get out of her seat. But as soon as she was out of the car she walked forcefully and with determination across the visitors' parking lot toward the front of the hospital. The large sign over the entrance doors was written in Greek: Πανεπιστημιακό Γενικό Νοσοκομείο Πατρών - Παναγία η Βοήθεια (General University Hospital of Patras - All Holy Theotokos the Helper).

"There are dogs over there," I pointed to the four dogs sleeping by a tree in the middle of a grassy patch a few meters away from the hospital's front doors. I had noticed the streetlights reflecting nicely on their wet and scruffy fur.

"Orphans! Hospital mixed-race dogs – they cry when someone dies," Mom explained. "Come on."

Mom bypassed the unoccupied information desk stopping for a minute to orient herself. She spotted the two elevators and walked eagerly towards them, ignoring my suggestions that we should talk to someone and not just go anywhere we wanted. An "Out of Service" sign was clearly in view on the right-hand elevator. She grabbed my hand and pulled me inside the other.

"I know where I am going," she insisted. "Come on."

The elevator stopped on the fourth floor. As the door opened we faced a long, rather dark hospital corridor with rows of rooms to the left and to the right.

"Room 412," Mom announced as she walked out of the

elevator leaving me behind.

To our left was an Exit door with trembling reddish light gleaming with phosphorescence the letters *Exodus*: through its small rectangular glass I could see a couple of people smoking. As I was reading the room numbers I noticed every room occupied by a few people—remarkable considering that it was past ten o'clock at night. Some took a long, distinct look at us as Mom clearly was looking impatient, irritated, and unhappy.

"Mαria mou (My Maria)...."

The scream came from a dark open space in the middle of the corridor. A shadow of a woman stood up from a couch.

"Maria mou...," this time it was a cry.

"Eleni mou (My Helen)...."

Mom and Auntie Eleni hugged and kissed, letting their tears freely roll down their cheeks. They kept repeating each other's names for a few seconds. Finally, mom took a breath.

"I have Leonartho with me. Angela will come on Monday. She could not come any sooner."

"Agape mou (My love)," Auntie said as she was giving me a big hug.

"Your uncle is leaving us. Your dearest uncle is leaving us." Two sentences filled with drama! Her tears were unstoppable. I held her close to my body. She had lost weight and her light brown hair was uncombed. Her skin felt dry and her eyes easily revealed many sleepless hours.

"Shhhh!" I whispered in her ear. "Don't worry. All would be okay. Where is he?"

She took us to room 412, the last room at the end of the corridor. A multi-patient room with four beds: three of them were surrounded by curtains hanging from the ceiling. One of them, bed #1, was occupied by Father Dimitri. Auntie introduced us to the priest and his two daughters who were visiting. One sat by his side on the bed and the other, on a chair by his headrest. Father Dimitri did not look like the Greek priests I knew. He had no beard or long hair. He was freshly shaved and his short hair was combed in a style that made him look in his late forties. Most likely he was much older.

"They just arrived from Canada," Auntie mournfully announced to them. "They made it to see my Yiorgo alive."

"Don't cry," Father Dimitri said. He raised his upper body and sat on his bed. His daughter held his hand in an attempt to support him and fixed his white pajamas to prevent them from becoming wrinkled. "Have faith. The Almighty loves us all."

I said hello in a hurry and moved on. For some reason, I knew my uncle was in bed #2. I moved the curtain to the side. My uncle's eyes were shut. He was breathing heavily from his mouth. His hands on top of the white bed sheet appeared lifeless. His right wrist was purple from the IV syringe delivering fluids to his body. His left hand was touching the metal bars of the raised bed-gate. I held his left palm in my hands and kissed his fingers gently.

"Uncle," I whispered gently closed to his ear. "Uncle.... It's me, Leonarthos. I came from Vancouver with *Mana*. She is here with me. Can you hear me?"

His fingers moved in my hands.

"Yiorgo mou, agape mou, is Leonarthos and your sister Maria," said Auntie. "They came from Canada to see you. Open your eyes agape mou to see them." Her words were loud, projected with determination. She was giving a direct order to the dying man.

I raised my head. Auntie and Mom were on the other side of the bed. Mom bent forward and kissed her brother on the cheek.

"Yiorgo mou," she begged. "It is me. Maria. Your sister. I came from Canada to see you. Open your eyes, Yiorgo mou."

I kissed my uncle on his forehead. Still holding his fingers I tried to project my words in an attempt to suffuse his eardrum.

"Uncle Yiorgo. We are here for you. Can you hear me?"

His head moved ever so slightly, indicating that he could hear me. His fingers twitched again.

"Yiorgo," Auntie insisted! "If you can hear us just move your eyelids."

Uncle George's eyelids moved much to the satisfaction of all of us. We were ecstatic. We had made it before he was gone forever. For just a second, the end was not so bad after all.

"Yiorgo," Mom said with tears rolling down once again. "Don't worry, Yiorgo mou. All would be okay."

His eyelids moved again. I felt his fingers moving stronger than before.

"He can hear you, *Mana*," I said. "He is moving his fingers."

"Good!" she said. "Let him rest. Thank God we came on time."

I left Mom and Auntie by his bedside and I went to find my aunt's cousin, Eleni. She was outside one of the Exit doors smoking, Auntie suggested, or perhaps down in the cafeteria to get some coffee as the cafeteria was closing soon. I could not miss her; surely I was going to remember her. We used to play together when she was fifteen and I was thirteen years old. And by the way, "She still has blonde hair. But it is colored."

I tried to remember how many cousins with the name Eleni my aunt had. Probably half a dozen; and what was going on in 1973 when I was thirteen? Uncle George and Aunt Eleni got married when I was eleven. When I was thirteen, Mom with my older brother, younger sister, and me, left our birth city of Kalamata. We moved to Oinoussai, a tiny island just a few kilometers away from Turkey and adjacent to the larger island of Chios. At around the same time, my father was debarking from his cargo ship, 'Lemos' in Vancouver, Canada. We stayed in Oinoussai until I was 18. That was when my parents decided for the family to immigrate to Vancouver.

"Eleni?" I was projecting my voice to the black skirt-wearing woman with her hair packed in some sort of a ponytail as she emerged from the side Exit door into the corridor.

"Yes… I am Eleni of Troy," she said playfully with a smile. "Hello little cousin," she continued.

She gave me a warm hug and kissed me on both cheeks. I kissed her cheeks as well, picking up the cigarette smell on her clothes and her skin.

"You know we are not really cousins," I said. "But who is arguing that? Can you please tell me what the heck is going on?"

She held my hand and led me into that little dark open space in the middle of the corridor, where I first saw Auntie. We sat on the couch. She told me about the stroke that my uncle suffered in his sleep almost a week ago. How Auntie almost suffered a breakdown trying to work things out between the hospital visits and caring for her old father, Panagiotis, at the same time. How Stavros, cousin Eleni's brother and his wife, Soula, took a handle of the situation when the health authorities moved my uncle to Patra, in an attempt to save his life. Soula stayed with Panagiotis in Kalamata. Stavros drove Auntie and his sister to Patra. He rented a couple of rooms in hotel, Galini, which was near the hospital. But there were no other rooms available in the hotel to reserve for Mom and me so he reserved a room in another hotel not far away.

"What a mess," she proclaimed. "All of a sudden the family's life went chaotic."

I listened without interrupting. I brought her hand to my lips and kissed it softly.

"Thank you for helping out my aunt. Where is the hotel? I would like to go with my mom and get some rest."

"The name of the hotel is Apollon and it's by the water. I have the directions," said Eleni. "Let's go to the room and see what's going on."

She held my hand all the way to the room. She hugged and kissed Mom, informed Auntie about some things that Stavros took care of, and gave me a piece of paper with the directions to the hotel. It took a little bit of a talk to persuade Mom to leave my uncle's bedside but eventually she agreed that she needed some rest.

The Hotel

The hotel was not far away from the hospital and as Eleni had pointed out, close to Patra's waterfront. Although the directions were good, it took me much longer to get to the hotel driving through the dark and wet night, in the small unfamiliar streets of that part of town. When we finally reached the three-level building Mom stopped for a minute to admire its lit marble steps that led to the small lobby.

Mrs. Toula Dendrinos, the owner of Apollon, was covering the night shift. She was a full-bodied woman around 50-ish. Her black, wavy hair floated freely down her shoulders. She was seated by one of the two tables centered in the lobby, watching a show on the TV hung in the lobby's wall across from the reception desk.

"Mrs. Maria and Leonarthos Hutchinson, I presume." Her voice was welcoming. She quickly stood up and moved behind the reception desk. "We were expecting you much sooner."

"Yes," I replied. "We made a stop in the hospital to see how my uncle is doing."

"Is he doing okay? Ms. Eleni said he was very sick."

"He is still alive," Mom said. "But who knows if he will survive the night."

"I wish you all the best," Mrs. Toula said awkwardly. "You folks had to come all the way from Canada. You must be exhausted. I booked room 102 on the first floor for you. It is a nice room with a street view but do not worry. It is not getting loud around here."

"We are not planning to spend our time in the room," Mom cut her off. "We just want to rest."

Mrs. Toula nodded her head in understanding and after the completion of the paperwork, she led the way up the stairs to the room, carrying Mom's suitcase. I carried mine, leaving Mom last to fight the stairs' gravity. Room 102 was a standard two single beds room by all accounts. Almost adjacent to the door was the washroom and the beds were separated by a small cabinet. The 48-inch TV across from the beds, flanked by a couple of pictures of fishing boats, covered a fair bit of the wall. A small balcony provided access to the outside and a view of the quiet street.

Mrs. Toula made sure that everything was to her satisfaction: she flushed the toilet, turned the TV on, started the heat, fluffed the pillows, and turned on the bed lights. Mom was quick to thank her and 'push' her out of the door, telling her to wake us up at seven a.m. Then Mom started unpacking her pajamas and toiletries from her suitcase.

I did not feel tired but I did feel depleted, if there is such a difference. I also unpacked my pajamas and washroom stuff. I took a rather cold shower. By the time Mom had her turn and came out of the washroom, I was already in bed watching TV. She tucked herself into the bed.

"Yiorgo mou," she whispered.

"Do not worry, *Mana*," I said. "Let's rest. Tomorrow is another day."

"Yes," she agreed. "Let's rest. Turn the TV off. Goodnight Leonarthe."

"Goodnight *Mana*."

I turned the TV off and closed my eyes. Finally, I was ready to get some rest.

"LEONARTHE!" Mom's scream was alarming.

I jumped off the bed. What time was it? What the heck was going on? The room's wall adjacent to the beds was vibrating. Was it an earthquake? But the floor was not shaking. I was lost in the sudden change from the night's peaceful persona. What was the moaning coming from the next room?

"ARE THEY HAVING SEX?"

I tried to focus! I turned on the bed light and took a good look at Mom. My face must have looked idiotic as I was still struggling to understand what was happening.

"ARE THEY HAVING SEX?" This time Mom's question produced a picture.

And the picture was getting clearer. The next room's occupants were having sex. He was moaning deeply and loud and she was encouraging him to penetrate her "harder and harder." And in all, their bed was moving, hitting the only wall separating us and them.

"Yes. They are," I finally said nervously. "I suppose they are having fun, *Mana*. I thought it was an earthquake."

"Oh my God!" she replied. "I came all the way from Canada and my brother is dying… and I am listening to two idiots having sex."

"Harder! Harder! Come now! Come now!" she screamed in English from the other side of the wall. And he did obey her, reaching his climax with a roaring sound.

Mom got up from her bed. "What a night, Panagia mou. (*She will often call the name of Maria, Mother of Jesus, All Holy Theotokos, aka Panagia, when distraught*). What a night!" she said in disbelief. "I hope they are done."

"I want more," the woman from next door said on cue with a catty crying tone. "I want more."

"What? She wants more? She got it hard and she wants more? IS SHE A NYMPHOMANIAC?" Mom banged the wall with her fists a couple of times angrily.

There was a few seconds of silence.

"I want more… more… more," the female voice demanded again, crying like a little child.

"YOU ARE NOT GOING TO GET MORE! HE HAD ENOUGH. LET US SLEEP." Mom shouted and banged the wall again.

"Leave them alone, *Mana*," I said. "They are done."

"I hope they are done," Mom pointed out angrily. "If she will not let us sleep I am going to knock on their door and pound their heads."

But there was silence from the next room. And I was drained. I said goodnight one more time to Mom and let my body relax under the bed covers. She decided that she could not sleep any longer and that she was going to watch TV.

The phone call from the hotel reception woke me up at 7 a.m. precisely. Mom was not in the room. I took another rather cold shower. My eyes were puffy and I felt drowsy. Eventually, I found Mom in the reception having coffee with Mrs. Toula. Last night's events were all summarized for Mrs. Toula and she insisted that this will not happen again as 'couples' who want to use the services of the hotel would not occupy the room adjacent to us.

Such small hotels often were used by guests to have one-night stands because the price was cheap – 25 euros per night, and if it was cash (no receipt required) you could get a room for 20 euros. Many Greeks were lucky enough to apply and get a loan from the government and through a European Community Program to start a hotel business. There were some criteria that needed to be met but most Greeks would tell you that anyone could go around them.

Uncle George told me, a few years back, that he was going to build a house in Trahila with the EU money. Trahila is the family village where Yannis and Katerina Thimouleas, my grandparents, were born and raised, and more than half of the old villagers had the same last name. The village is located at the bottom of the Messinian gulf and it is the very last one at the end of the small, snaky road by the feet of Mountain Taygetos. It is a wonderful picture-perfect village with a chewed-out rock in the middle of the small port, prominently rising from the seawater. It looks like a 'Trahilos,' the villagers will tell you and thus the name of the village. In fact, rumour has it that Paris, the Trojan Prince, used this small port to 'steal' Helen, the wife of King Agamemnon to Troy. Hence, that triggered the Trojan War.

It was easy to get a loan, Uncle insisted. The only thing he had to prove was that the house was used as a hotel for the first two years or so. Then he could claim it as his own. And he could also make money as he had many friends who wanted to spend time in the village, especially in the summers. He could charge them a cheap rate and at the same time he could also use the house for his own pleasure.

To the point that the EU had provided the money to the Greek government and someday the money had to be paid back, Uncle would laugh at. As far as he was concerned we were talking about free money. And on another point, that Greeks needed to pay taxes and when someone was renting his place he had to charge the applicable taxes and return them to the government, Uncle was quick to point out that no one does this. I went to Canada and became paranoid, he remarked. In fact, "Canadians are like sheep that follow other sheep and let the government take all of their money in taxes to take care of drug addicts." That was, at least, part of my uncle George's view of Canada.

"Oh, the lovebirds are coming for breakfast," Mrs. Toula said as she got up from her chair to go behind the reception desk.

I changed my posture to take a look at the couple coming down the stairs. She was an attractive 20-ish blonde with her wet-looking hair combed into a ponytail. She had a slim body and wore a black miniskirt to show off her curves. Her naked long legs ended in black high heels. Her companion was good looking, dressed in jeans and his white t-shirt exaggerated his muscular upper body. His black, curly hair ended short of his shoulders.

"Good morning," she said as she passed by us. They occupied the other table in the lobby. She crossed her legs, revealing much of her white, unblemished skin.

"I bet you want more." Mom whispered between her lips.

Mrs. Toula brought them the standard 'English' breakfast and rested the tray on the coffee table in front of them.

"How was your sleep?" she asked them.

"Fabulous," the young woman replied in a joyful manner. "I just love it here."

I spotted an accent with her Greek. Greek-American perhaps?

"Of course, it was fabulous. She wanted more, the 'poutana'," Mom whispered just loud enough for me to hear. "Finish up your breakfast, Leonarthe, so we can go to the hospital. I will throw my coffee in her lap if we stay much longer here."

"Why don't you go upstairs to freshen up, *Mana*?" I suggested. "When you come down we can go."

"Alright! You have ten minutes. I need to go and visit my brother. We should have been in the hospital already. We wasted too much time."

"Hi. My name is Lita," the young woman introduced herself to me as Mom was climbing the stairs. "Are you guys here on holidays?"

I turned toward her. I brought the coffee cup to my lips and slurped the hot liquid before I spoke.

"No. My uncle is in the hospital, seriously sick. We came from Vancouver last night. We are heading to Kalamata."

"Vancouver? Canada? I am from Los Angeles. My dad is Greek. I am here on holidays and I love it because all the tourists are gone and I am the only one around. I know Kalamata. I was there a few years ago and I enjoyed everything about the city," she said in English and with excitement.

I smiled. I could not help but interpreting her words with a sexual meaning. I offered my hand to shake hers.

"My name is Leonardo, Lita. Nice to meet you…," I replied in English.

"Leonardo Da Vinci… Leo for short?" She looked at her companion but he did not bother to engage. Instead he picked up a newspaper from the shelf under the coffee table and started to read.

"I suppose he does not speak English?" I said, glancing his way.

"He understands a few words. But do not hold this against him. He is good in other things," she said jokingly.

"Hm! He understands the word 'harder' I think," I said sarcastically.

Her face went blank all of a sudden and for a few seconds. But then she figured it out.

"OH NO! It was you guys banging the wall?" In one move, she bent forward and with both hands gathered her miniskirt between her slightly opened legs in an attempt to cover herself. She giggled like a little girl.

"Yes. You produced an earthquake, Lita," I said with a

smile. "My mom wanted to come and club you… especially when you were asking for more."

She giggled again. Her ponytail flipped sideways. Her blue eyes peeked at me curiously through her hair. She rearranged herself in the chair, leaving most of her slim legs open to view. She took the biscotti from the plate and brought it to her lips. Was she enjoying the conversation? She turned to face him.

"Lover," she said in Greek, taking a small bite at the same time. "We need to be less noisy."

He did not reply. With a sideways glance at me, he quickly refocused his eyes back on the paper, flipping his hair to the side with a sudden jerk of his head. It looked like he was reading a Sports page. That's serious reading for a Greek man.

"Next time I will keep quiet Leooo," she said teasingly putting emphasis to the vowel 'o'.

I could tell she did not mean it but I was not in a hurry to argue this point. I took another sip of my coffee, using it as an excuse to stop the conversation. Mom was coming down the stairs anyway. I said goodbye to Lita and wished her well.

"What did the masochist say to you?" Mom asked while boarding the car.

"Wow, *Mana*. Are there any other names you can call her? Forget about her. Should we stop to get some desserts for the folks in the hospital? You know, the priest and the other folks who occupy the other beds?" She nodded in agreement.

She drifted into silence during the drive to the hospital. The brightness of the day's sky added to the town's liveliness. She allowed me to decide what desserts to get from the small cafeteria called 'Orexi', located a few blocks away from the hospital.

"Church bells… is it something happening this Saturday?" I asked the young girl working in the café.

"These are the bells from the hospital chapel," she replied calmly as if this happened all the time and was not an issue. "Probably someone died."

As I got behind the wheel, Mom urged me to hurry.

"The chapel bells were going. I hope my brother is okay. Yiorgo mou…." She made the sign of the cross and started a prayer.

*

The Hospital—The Death

We found Auntie seating alone in the corridor. Mom and Auntie hugged and kissed and cried again when they saw each other. Auntie filled us in while we indulged ourselves over the desserts. Uncle George fell into a coma late last night. The massive stroke he had suffered in his sleep a few days ago had enormous negative consequences in his brain cells, depriving them of oxygen. The chief doctor in charge wanted to pull the plug but Auntie wanted to wait for Mom to be present before "letting Yiorgo go." The chief doctor would come back again at some point in the afternoon. Eleni was with her brother Stavros, taking care of plans to take the body back to Kalamata and making funeral arrangements.

During the night the occupant in bed #4 had a stroke and hospital staff could not save him. He had no family. He was sixty-two years old. There was a small service for him in the church in the morning. So sad! Father Dimitri was dismissed and he said, "God bless you all."

Stefanos, the occupant of bed #3 was recovering from his ulcer surgery. We did not meet him last night as he was recovering but he knew we were from Canada and was eager to meet us.

From my view of the corridor I saw Eleni and Stavros walking toward us.

"Hi everybody," Eleni announced their arrival. "I brought Stavros with me."

I last saw Stavros in 2007. I was going through some major marital issues and he was influential in helping me to reconsider divorcing my wife and to give it another go for the sake of the children. One of his philosophical statements was that, "Women go crazy when they have kids. Having two young ones after 40 probably changed your wife's hormones and that is why she is going nuts. You are a good man Leo and hopefully she will see the lighting after the thunder." Stavros would often make such comments laughingly, making the thick moustache, which covered most of his upper lip, tremble.

I agreed with some of his comments but deep inside I knew that my marriage problems were not a joke. My wife was drinking heavily and her jealousy was unbearable. At times, she accused me endlessly of having affairs, not only with other women but men as well. Her vulgar and abusive language was negatively impacting my overall health.

Stavros, at 5 foot 6, with his stocky and rugged body, was a farmer since the early years of his life. He had great manners and was always willing to help others. When his sister Eleni got married at 16 and her alcoholic husband became abusive, Stavros followed the relationship closely, helping her out every way he could even more so, when her husband passed away a few years later from— liver cancer.

His moustache, still thick and black, did not bother Mom when he kissed her cheeks. He shook my hand and with his crisp heavy voice, announced to Auntie that everything was arranged.

"I had an issue with the booking of the funeral date," he

said apologetically. "The first available date is this coming Thursday. I took it, but I also put us on a waitlist."

"What kind of waitlist are you talking about? Like, if somebody died, the funeral will get cancelled?" I said in disbelief.

"Yes. Apparently, a scheduled funeral may not proceed because relatives get sick, or something else is happening in the household. I don't know. But that's what the church person said," Stavros answered with a serious tone.

Everybody seemed to understand the issue except me. Notwithstanding my confusion, we finally entered the room to check on my uncle.

Uncle's eyes were still shut. His breathing from his open mouth was heavy and slow. The machine and the IVs that he was hooked up to before were removed. His hands lay on the bed, palms down, by his side. Mom kissed his forehead. She and Auntie sat in the two available chairs by the bed while the rest of us stood on the other side. I went to the window and took a look outside. Four levels below in the half-empty parking lot the weak sunrays were reflecting backward to the sky. And by the trees, a couple of hospital dogs were napping. I opened the window a couple of inches to allow some fresh air in and battle the foul smell of illness lingering in the room. For a few minutes there was silence in the room.

"Hey. Hello?" The voice came from bed #3.

I pulled the curtain open partway around bed #3 and took a look at the man seated halfway upright, with a couple of pillows supporting his upper body. He was bald and his facial skin was covered with scabs making him look in his seventies.

"Can I help you?" I asked the question courteously but really I was not interested in helping anyone at that time.

"Hey, I am Stefanos. How is he doing?"

"He is dying, Stefane. He is dying," Auntie replied as she hid her face in her palms.

"Ela. Ela. Be strong!" Mom said, patting Auntie's shoulders. Cousin Eleni moved to their side and stroked Auntie's hair with her fingers.

Stefanos looked at me at a loss. He signaled me to close the curtain, inviting me to sit in the chair by his bedside.

"I used to be a sailor. Your aunt said you are from Vancouver. I have a cousin in Vancouver. Michalis is his name. Do you know him? I have not seen him in years."

I felt a hysterical laugh try to escape but managed a smile.

"No. I know a couple of Michalis' in Vancouver, Stefane. Have you been to Vancouver?"

"No. But I know it's close to Toronto. They are saying it is very cold."

"Well, it gets very cold in the winter in Toronto. That's true.... Vancouver not so much. And it's on the other side of Canada by the Pacific Ocean."

"Yes, I know. Close to Montreal right?"

I decided not to give Stefanos a lesson in geography. After all he used to be a sailor. Who knows? He may have known of a Vancouver close to Montreal and Toronto.

"My cousin Michalis was a cook in a Greek restaurant," he said.

"What is his last name? Do you know the name of the restaurant?"

"His last name is Georgopoulos. He is younger than I am. He is 55 or 56 or 57. I don't know the name of the restaurant. But I know he lived in an apartment close to the water."

I decided to stretch the truth. "You know Stefane. I know such a Michali. He works at Oreste's restaurant in

Vancouver for quite a few years now."

Felix Hutchinson, with dual Canadian and British citizenships, came to Athens from Vancouver Canada, in January 20, 1979 with a broken right arm covered in plaster to help his wife Maria and his three children: Ioannis of age twenty, Leonarthos of age eighteen, and Angela of age thirteen, to immigrate to Canada. There were two major problems with his children's nationality. The first one was that young Greek men when they reach the age of eighteen had to serve in the army for two years. The second one was that the children had no passports.

The first problem got solved easily. Greek government officials denounced the children as being Greek citizens although they were born and lived all of their lives in Greece. Simply, Felix was not Greek. That Maria was Greek was irrelevant. In fact, the children were recorded in the Greek 'books' as 'foreigners' with a Trinidad and Tobacco nationality; and British subjects. No foreigners were allowed to serve in the Greek army.

The second problem was decisively more complex. Felix and his older brother Sonny, were born in Trinidad and Tobacco, a British colony. Their father, a British dentist named Leonard Hutchinson, had an affair with his home care taker, Angela Mayo, a local woman. The affair, considered illegal at the time (he was of a high class and she was not), was kept in secret. Later on, when Felix was sixteen years old, his father recognized him and Sonny as his two legal sons. So the name Felix Mayo Hutchinson was written in a British passport.

Felix had to work in cooperation with the Canadian and British embassies to get a one-time temporary British passport for his three children. Finally, along with his two sons, he arrived in Vancouver in February 1, 1979. Maria and Angela were to arrive in July of the same year after the end of the school year.

Felix had a two-bedroom apartment in Kitsilano since 1974. Kitsilano was the area where most Greek immigrants settled because it was by the Burrard Inlet's waterfront overlooking across the water the large skyscrapers in Vancouver's downtown. Ioannis started working right *away with his father as a custodian in the United Way building by Fir and 7th street. Leonarthos' first job as a 'fresh off the boat' 18-year-old young adult was at Oreste's restaurant on Broadway Street. Until its closure in 1989, Oreste's was one of the busiest Greek restaurants in Vancouver. His initial work was to prepare Greek salads on demand for $3.25 per hour. Later, he worked with the head cook named Michali preparing all the required menu items.*

Michali was a middle-aged uneducated immigrant from Athens and father of three children: two daughters and a son. He was a drug abuser in his early life in Greece and as a result of this his thinking process was slower than normal. He would often repeat two stories. One was that one time he had sex with his wife. After he had an orgasm he kept going. His wife finally said. "Stop pounding. Are you going to make it a tzatziki?" The other story was about how he was successful in finally having a son. "I had two daughters and I wanted to have a son to name him George after my father. So, I talked to an old Greek woman. She sold me a special potato for one hundred dollars. She told me to put it under my pillow and to have sex when the moon was full. And it worked!"

"Hey, when you go back can you tell him to write or call me?" Stefanos said. "I wrote my information for him in case he does not have it any longer."

He searched under one of the pillows and withdrew a small yellow paper. On it he had written his name, phone number, and address, ending with the sentence: "With love your cousin, Stefanos. You know, the one who used to beat you all the time when we were kids. Ha! Ha! Ha!"

He passed me the paper telling me to give it to Michali along with his good wishes.

I felt guilty. "You know Stefane, I will try my best. But if I will not find Michali, I will let you know. Is that okay?"

"Yes. Thank you. Thank you so much. And what's your name again?"

"Leo."

He took both my hands in his hands and pulled me toward him. He gave me a hug and wished me good luck. I thanked him. He was clearly emotional. I closed the curtain behind me just in time, I thought, as the chief doctor and his entourage of four student doctors entered the room.

He approached Uncle's bed and introduced himself to Mom and me as "Master Surgeon, Mr. Sotirakos". He raised Uncle's eyelids, took a fast look with the help of his small flashlight, and closed them again. He lifted the white bed sheet and took a look at the feet before checking the hands for a pulse. He finally addressed Mom and Auntie.

"It is nothing else that we can do. At this stage we removed all the machines that were keeping him alive and we are letting him decide when it is time to go."

"Mr. Sotirakos. How long before he leaves us?" Mom asked.

"I don't know. Perhaps one or two days tops? His heart is very strong but his organs are failing him. Right now he is in a coma and that has slowed down his metabolism. If we do not provide him with nutrients he will not last for too long. But who knows? At least he is not suffering."

"Would it be possible to give him a morphine shot and let him go?" I suggested.

He took a long, astonishing look at me, showing some disgust.

"We do not kill people in this hospital, sir," he said sharply in English with a strong accent. "We are not in Canada."

"It has nothing to do with Canada," I replied in English. "If he is going to die why is it necessary to put everyone in despair for however long this may take? And why use unnecessary hospital resources?"

He did not bother to reply. He moved by the door where the students were and started talking to them rather secretly. They were nodding their heads in agreement. Was he talking to them about what I said? Or about how Canadian doctors kill their patients?

"Was this one with the stiletto shoes taking care of our Yiorgo?" I heard Mom saying quietly to Auntie and Eleni.

"I heard in the cafeteria that she always says, 'YES' to the doctors," Eleni said, covering her mouth with her right hand to allow only us who were close by to hear her.

I took another look at the student doctors. One of them, a good-looking brunette was wearing stiletto shoes. Her white hospital robe, open at the top, revealed much of her breasts. The robe was barely covering her actual miniskirt. Her make-up, inviting, highlighted her cheekbones and her lips were finished with red lipstick. My first thought was that she came out of a 'massage' parlor or that she was an actress in a porno hospital movie.

Auntie whispered, "You should have been here when she was examining our Yiorgo. She was bending over him to listen to his heart with her stethoscope and her breasts were all over him. I said, 'Open your eyes Yiorgo mou to see what you are missing. Ela agape mou open your eyes.'"

"Did she hear you?" I asked.

"Of course she did," she added. "She rearranged her bra and then she took the plastic tube out of his penis."

All three of them giggled like little schoolgirls. I suppose the miracle did not happen as Uncle did not open his eyes. I asked Stavros to take the women to the cafeteria so that Mom could eat something. I was full after eating the desserts and I also wanted to stay with Uncle and decompress a little in my own thoughts. They left soon after.

"Hey Leo! Can you open the curtain for me?" Stefanos

called.

I did. Then I went back and sat in the chair by Uncle's headrest.

"I know he was a sailor as well," Stefanos said. "I was a sailor since I was sixteen years old. I retired a few years back."

"My uncle finished the marine academy when he was sixteen," I said. "He was a mechanic in the cargo ships. He left the sea in the seventies to become a mechanic at the Karelia tobacco factory in Kalamata."

"I remember the last time I embarked the ship called 'Amalia'. We were going from Japan to America and we encountered a really bad weather. I said, 'Panagia mou, if I will live through this I will never set foot on another ship.'"

I thought I heard my uncle moving. I excused myself from Stefano and turned around. Uncle George's breathing became heavier, with a few seconds pause between each breath he took. It certainly looked like he was battling something. I touched his forehead. It felt cold. I leaned close to his head and whispered in his ear, "Let go Uncle. It's okay. Don't be afraid. Let go."

A couple of seconds or so passed. His last breath came out as a deathly hush and disappeared in the room's silence. I was at ease. I kissed his forehead and placed his hands, one on top of the other, on his chest. I pulled the bed sheet over his head.

"Is he gone?" Stefanos asked.

"Yes," I replied.

"He is in God's hands now," he said. "He may rest in peace."

"I am going to get my family, Stefane, from the cafeteria. If anyone comes please pass the information that my uncle passed away and that we will be back right away."

"Yes. Don't worry. GO! GO!"

As I was leaving the room, the dogs' howling reached me from the parking lot below and through the window's slim opening. The three women and Stavros somehow knew what happened when they saw me entering the cafeteria. Did they also hear the dogs? They followed me back to the room quietly after I told them that "Uncle Yiorgo passed away." Auntie and Mom started sobbing when they saw the bed sheet covering the whole body. Stavros uncovered his face. All four of them kissed Uncle's forehead.

Suddenly the silence was interrupted by Auntie Eleni's hysterical and repeating cry. "My Yiorgo left me. My Yiorgo left me. What am I going to do now?"

I could hear again the dogs' howling. Stefanos calling to "Have courage" across the room was mixed with Mom calling her brother's name while looking at his stony face. Eleni and Stavros hugged Auntie.

I placed my hand on Mom's shoulder, thinking: *It is better this way. Who wants to be around a person in a coma for days to come with no revival whatsoever? Uncle George wouldn't. I am sure of that. I just need to keep quiet and let them calm down on their own. I need to stay strong.*

It took a while for everyone to calm down and get a strong hold of their emotions. I took Stavros outside the room and I told him that I would go to the hotel to check out and come back as soon as I could. He also had to go to their hotel and do the same. We agreed that we would meet in the parking lot, put Auntie's and Eleni's luggage in my car, and then I would drive the women to Kalamata.

Episode 4

The Drive to Kalamata

I went back to the hotel to check out. Mrs. Toula gave me her sympathies when she heard the news.

"Good luck! Say hello to your mom," she called from the steps of the hotel when I was driving away. "We are all going to die."

That's reassuring I thought. What a comment. Of course, we are all going to die. Even the sun will die after a few billion light years. So who cares? For us humans, when the time comes, we do care. There were a few times that Uncle George had talked to me about death. He was 15 years older than Auntie and his view was that he would live for many years to keep up with my aunt's youth. But of course, one day he was bound to die admirably.

In one of our discussions, he was worrying about what would happen to Auntie if he died. Probably, "She would do hara-kiri," he said laughingly.

I did point out that, "Sometimes we do not know when our time is up. Perhaps Auntie Eleni would die first and then he would do hara-

kiri. Or perhaps they may both die together in a car accident, which by the way, they almost did when they were newlyweds on their drive to Trahila."

"Yes, we rolled 40 or so meters down the cliff in the mountain and I only got some scratches— your aunt broke her arm, and her little niece suffered a few bruises. I climbed the cliff and stopped a car. The folks helped us. No one believed that we escaped death then," he said enthusiastically.

But overall, he was adamant that he would die in his sleep without suffering like Persari.

"Do you remember her? When you were a kid you used to help her a lot."

Yes, I remembered Persari. Her actual name was Persephone. She was my Yiayia's sister, never being married, and betrayed by a man whom she loved very much. In her old age and when she became sick, her immediate family abandoned her except Yiayia, who gave her one room to stay rent-free. As a six-year-old, I used to go into her room to feed her and wash her face. She would often complain of the flies landing on her "old skin", so she would ask me to spray her face with the 'aerosol' canister so that the flies' eggs would not germinate. In her final weeks, I was not allowed to visit her any longer and witness her suffering, for apparently, she suffered a lot.

I met Stavros in the parking lot. We put Auntie's and Eleni's bags in my car. Three bags all-together. Stavros explained to me that it would be better if I took the newly constructed road to Kalamata.

"The road goes by Olympia, and then connects to the National Highway that leads to Tripoli, and then continues down to Kalamata. But I am warning you to pay attention to the road signs because if you miss the connector exit then you will get lost."

"I have been to Olympia before but from the coastal road through Pyrgos and Zacharo, Stavros."

"Taking that route is also okay but you need to pay attention for the connector exit after the village of Kalo Nero to connect to the National Highway. If you miss the connector the road would take you all the way down to Pilos. From there you can get to Kalamata but the road is through the mountains. If you miss that connector, the road would take you to Methoni around the first leg of the Peloponnese to Foinikounda and then Petalidi and then to Kalamata. This is a very long ride and don't do it."

The three women and I left Stavros in Patra to take care of the legalities. With Mom and Auntie in the back of the car and Eleni occupying the passenger's front seat, I drove through the city of Patra and stopped in a gas station to fill-up just before taking the exit to the National Highway. Everyone was silent for quite a long time but eventually Eleni broke the silence.

"Which way are you going Leo?" she asked softly.

"I want to take the road to Olympia. But I am not familiar with it. I am familiar with taking the coastal road. But Stavros said it will take longer for us to reach Kalamata."

"Just go the way you know," Mom reassured me.

"So what's going on between you and your wife?" Eleni begged to start a conversation. "I heard that she is very jealous and she drinks a lot."

"I don't know where you heard this but it's true. I am struggling to keep up with her accusations that I am having affairs with other women."

"Are you?"

The question bothered me. I took an ardent look at her. I didn't like the idea that she did not trust me.

"No. I have no time for extra trouble, TROY. My job as an Acting Principal is not easy and at the same time, I am coaching three soccer teams. And I am dealing with so many health issues with Marialina. You know, my special needs child…."

She looked straight into my eyes. She realized how she had upset me with her question.

"I would have been jealous of you," she said. "You are beautiful. And you know, I like it when you call me Troy."

I eased up, relaxing my grip on the steering wheel.

"Eleni, a little jealousy goes long ways," I replied calmly. "But over the top jealousy it's a disease. And my wife, I think, she has 'Attention Deficit Disorder'. But what bothers me the most is that she would not say thank you or agree with anything I say or do. She is mostly negative, vulgar, and, at times, physical and abusive. Now, if I was a woman, people would support me. But since I am a man, most folks would call me a 'pussy' if I dared to complain. Do you understand what I am saying?"

She took a deep breath and started telling me her story. How she got married at sixteen, how her husband was an alcoholic and abusive, and how she decided to suck it up to protect her young daughter.

"When my husband died I went into the church and lit a candle to Panagia, the Holy Theotokos, for hearing me out." She put her right hand's fingers together and made the sign of the cross, bringing her hand from her forehead to her stomach to her right shoulder, and then to her left shoulder. "Oh Mother of Jesus, thank you," she said repeating the hand movement three times.

She continued outlining her struggles as a young woman with a child.

"All the Greek men assumed I was easy and desperate for sex. I could not go out of the house without having jerks following me. I have not been with a man for quite a few years, you know. Actually, I don't remember the last time a man held me other than the men in my family."

I was not planning to judge her but she did become informative, closing with the point that all her life now is about her grandson—the son of her only daughter.

"You know, Troy. In Kalamata, I will hold you every day as long as you want."

"Ah," she said taking my hand in hers laughingly. "That would be lovely, little cousin, but why wait until Kalamata?"

"Where are we now? It is getting dark really fast," Mom's voice surprised me. I thought she was asleep.

"We are approaching Pyrgos, *Mana*. Not too bad so far. A little bit of traffic. Should I stop for you guys to rest?"

"No. No. Keep going Leonarthe. We will stop when we get to Kalamata," said Auntie. Another surprise! She too was awake.

I found a radio station playing classical music. The women seemed to relax in their seats. I was relaxed too but something was telling me that I needed to pay attention for the connector exit of Kalo Nero.

A couple of hours later I posed the question, "Did we pass Kalo Nero?"

No answer. The women were asleep. Oh well, I thought to myself. Who cares? I will keep going and at Pilos, I will take the exit toward Kalamata. One hour later Eleni woke up.

"Are we close to Kalamata yet?" she asked while stretching.

"No. I came all the way down to Pilos and now I am driving through the mountains toward Kalamata. We should be there in an hour or so."

Eleni spotted uneasiness in my voice.

"What's wrong?" she asked.

"Well, awhile back I was following a wide road with four

lanes. Now the road is only two lanes. And I passed a junction that had no signs pointing to Kalamata. So I guessed which way to continue. And my phone is dead. I cannot check maps or anything…."

"My phone is not dead but there is no reception here in no man's land," Eleni said checking her phone. She turned to take a look behind her. "Should we wake them-up?"

"No leave them. I have been watching the moon and following it for some time now. But I keep going up and down various mountains. I think I am lost."

She took a look at the clear sky. The moon was a huge circle full of light.

"Wow. The moonbeam is so beautiful, Leonarthe. It is a full moon. It is so beautiful."

"Yes. But I am lost."

"You cannot get lost in Greece," she said with a laugh. "Eventually you will come across the Mediterranean Sea."

"True. But we left Patra four hours or so ago and still no Kalamata. And it's so freaking dark. We are the only car on the road and the only thing around us is thousands of olives trees that look one million years old and scary in the dark. At least the olive trees tell me we are in the Messinia area but where in Messinia? We are getting down to the last quarter of the gasoline tank and we better stop somewhere to ask for directions. And I need to empty my bladder as well."

"Me too!" she said. "Hey, look here is a village. What church is this?"

"The sign said the church of Agia Kyriaki. Here is a taverna and… it is of course open at ten o'clock at night. Perfect."

There are two kinds of villages in Greece, as far as I am concerned. The ones that are built around a road with a church in a central location and ones that are at the end of a road with a church in a central location.

In the first case, the road splits the village in two: the North and South or the East and West. In the second case, the road ends at the start of the village. In both cases, a taverna or a coffee shop and other local businesses are pretty much in the centre of the village with the houses spread all around.

I stopped the car in the only available parking lot by the steps of the taverna named Kataraktis (*Waterfall*). I left the job to Eleni to wake up Mom and Auntie and explain to them what was happening. I proceeded inside the taverna. One table was occupied by a middle-aged man with a t-shirt slightly pulled over his stomach showing a hairy belly. On another table, there were two kids around ten years old watching TV. Behind the tiny bar, an overweight woman, probably in her sixties, welcomed me.

"Could you please tell me where the washroom is located?" I asked her.

"The men's washroom is outside around the back by the tree. The women's washroom is inside the kitchen to the left."

I thanked her and went outside. The women were coming out of the car. I stopped for a second to address them.

"Women's washroom is inside the kitchen to the left."

I disappeared around the building's corner. The cool almost dry moonbeam was giving enough light for me to see that there was no 'jiffy' anywhere for me to do my business. The only thing between some bushes and a couple of abandoned stables was a huge and magnificent maple tree covering an enormous amount of atmosphere. It took me a minute to think. And then I 'watered' the tree.

I found the women inside the taverna seated by the kids' table drinking beverages. As I headed towards them I passed the man, who whispered something.

"Yes?" I posed the one-word question without expecting

an answer.

"Can you spare a woman?" he asked, flipping with his tongue a toothpick hanging from the tips of his lips.

"Sure," I said all serious. "Which one do you want?"

"What about the young one?"

"Sure." I turned toward Eleni. "TROY... Are you available?"

Eleni stared at us. She said nothing but her fist came up giving the Italian 'salute' to me and the man. I laughed aloud and then went to talk to the woman behind the bar.

"That was the best pee ever. I hope your directions how to get to Kalamata would be as straightforward as your directions to the washroom."

She looked puzzled, not understanding my sarcasm. She gave me directions how to, "Drive straight until the road splits. Take the left road and go up the mountain and then down the mountain. Be careful of wild animals. *("What wild animals? Greeks have eaten them all," Auntie said, between the laughs of Mom and Troy, when I relayed what the taverna woman told me).* You will go through a gravel road because the government did not have money to finish it and they left it. What a disgrace. Not even buses go through that road any longer. The gravel road connects to the National Road of Pilos-Kalamata. Just follow the signs. If there are no signs keep to the right. Kalamata is to our right from here."

We left the taverna but not without Troy calling the man a pervert. He did not seem to care. He opened his legs wide, showing his hairy belly even more, and told her that he loved her and wanted her. She was about to attack him but I held her back while Mom and Auntie remained flabbergasted by his remarks. I urged them all to ignore him and literally pushed them out of the door and onto the street.

One hour later, we were on the outskirts of Kalamata.

Soon after, I was parking the car in front of Auntie's five-levelled apartment building. Soula, Stavros's wife, was having a smoke on the fifth floor's balcony. She spotted us and started yelling.

"Oh my God! We thought you were in an accident. We were expecting you two hours ago. Come in. Come in. The door is open."

"I want to go to my house," Mom said. "Sister-in-law, go upstairs and rest. We will talk in the morning."

It was agreed. I followed Mom around the corner of the three-levelled apartment building adjacent to Auntie's. She led me to the back of the building following the guiding moonlight and started climbing up the small stairs rounding a central cemented pillar. Carrying two suitcases, it was not easy for me to maneuver between the iron railing and the pillar but I made it to the third floor a few seconds behind her. Mom had opened the penthouse's kitchen door and had turned the lights on. Everything was in order and to her approval since Soula had prepared the two-bedroom penthouse for us. I dropped the suitcases in the living room, saying goodnight to Mom as I entered the room with the two single beds. With my clothes on, I fell asleep as soon as my body hit the bed.

The Church of Ascension

The church where my uncle's funeral was to take place was Ekklisia Analipsi (Church of Ascension). Its address is 24101 Messinias Street in Kalamata and it is built in the square that finishes the South end of Analipseos Street. The church has an abundance of empty cemented space around it, limited only by Mpoumpoulinas Street in the East, by Evaggelistrias Street in the West, and by Messinias Street in the North.

Orthodox faithful or visitors who enter the main entrance will find the collection box where they can get candles by donation. The candles can then be placed in one of the two large brass candle stands called 'menalia', placed on either side of the Royal Doors, in the middle of the wooden portal in the narthex (the connection between the Church and the outside world). The portal has many icons but the main icon is this painting of Jesus Resurrection and Ascension.

The Royal Doors connect the narthex to the nave (the main body of the church where the people stand during the services). The priest goes through the Royal Doors in the name of Christ The Savior before starting any services.

Analipsi has no pews but there are seats available, and along the walls *stacidia* (high-armed chairs with armrests high enough to be used for support while standing). Traditionally, there is no sitting during services with the only exceptions being during the reading of the Psalms, and the priest's sermon. The people stand before God.

Analipsi's walls are covered from floor to ceiling with icons and wall paintings of saints, depicting their lives and many stories from the Bible. Men and women stand separately in the nave with men standing on the right and women on the left. With this arrangement, it is emphasized that people are all equal before God (equal distance from the altar), and that the man is not superior to the woman.

Above the nave, the large dome weighs down in the middle of the rectangular- shaped building. This particular shape has a linear layout with side-aisles, in an attempt to relate to the faithful, the concept that the Church is the Ark of Salvation (as in Noah's Ark), in which the world is saved from the flood of temptations. All around the dome there are icons, depicting Jesus's Apostles. In the middle of the dome and as high as possible from the ground, there is the painting of God, The Father And Almighty, (Παντοκρατωρ/Pantokrator, 'Ruler of All'), with his Finger pointing toward the only direction offered to humanity. The heavens!

The huge polyeleos (chandelier) hanging from the middle of the dome distributes its rich light everywhere in the open church spaces. Yet, the sunrays that get through the many multicolor glass mural windows produce a wonderful ambience. Some of the sunrays get reflected back to the bell tower, which is a separate building in the western part of the church.

Analipsi's iconostasis, also called the τεμπλον/templon, follows the classic architecture of mid-17th-century Orthodox churches. Its screen or wall between the nave and the sanctuary is covered with icons. There are three doors: one in the middle and one on either side. The central one, called the Beautiful Gate, is only used by the clergy. The doors on either side are called the Deacons' Doors or Angel Doors as they depict on them the Archangels Michael and Gabriel. These doors are used by deacons and servers to enter the sanctuary. To the right of the Beautiful Gate, as viewed from the nave, there is the icon of Christ and the icon of St. John the Baptist; to the left is the icon of Theotokos holding her Son, Christ. There are many other icons on Analipsi's iconostasis depicting Prophets, the Great Feast, the Apostles, and the Holy Trinity.

The area behind the iconostasis, reached through the Beautiful Gates or Angel Doors, is the church's sanctuary or altar with the altar table or holy table or throne occupying the central area. There is also the apse containing the high place at the centre back of the altar with a throne for the bishop and the synthronos, or seats for the priests on either side; the Chapel of Prothesis, on the north side, where the offerings are prepared in the *Proskomedia* before being brought to the altar table and the holy vessels are stored; and the *Diaconicon*, on the south side of the altar, where the vestments are stored.

Analipsi's altar is square with a heavy brocade outer covering that reaches all the way to the floor. Atop the altar table, at the centre towards the back, is an ornate container, the tabernacle, where the reserved Eucharistic elements are stored for communion. It is shaped like a model of a church building. In front of this, and under a folded piece of cloth—called the *eiliton*, the priest settles the Gospel book with its decorated gold plated cover. Folded within the *eiliton* is the *antimension*, which is a silken cloth, imprinted with a depiction of the burial of Christ and with relics sewn into it. Both these cloths are unfolded before the offerings are placed on the altar table. Behind the altar is a seven-branched candlestick, which recalls the seven-branched candlestick of the Old Testament Tabernacle and Temple in Jerusalem. Behind this is a golden processional cross. On either side of the cross are *hexapteryga (liturgical fans)*, which represent the six-winged Seraphim. Against the wall, behind the altar, is a large cross with a flat iconographic depiction of Christ (corpus), which can be removed during the 50 days following Pascha (Easter).

Day One After Death

I woke up to the sound of church bells. It took me a few minutes to orient myself, fighting my thinking that I was still in Patra. Mom left me a note in the kitchen to go upstairs to Auntie's apartment. I did not rush myself, taking time to unpack my suitcase and take a shower. I decided to wear my Adidas soccer pants and a T-shirt. The TV in the living room was not working. I pulled the large, glassy double doors apart and walked onto the balcony. The November sun was beaming with pride in the middle of the sky with only a couple of thin clouds daring him to make them disappear. Right across, on the other side of Psaron Street, Kalamata's Municipal Railway Park served as a museum for old train engines. Most of its surrounding trees were occupied by hundreds of birds chirping along with the church bells. I stretched my arms and took a deep breath.

"LEONARTHE."

The shout came from up high. I spotted Eleni smoking

on the balcony a couple of floors higher from where I was. I looked past her. Right behind her, the massive building called *Mylos* (mill), reminded me of the many playdates I had in its empty floors when I was a child. The building covered half of the block squared by the four streets: Ieroloxiton, Trion Navarchon, Idras and Psaron Street, which is a one-way street from the city's Centre to Likourgou Street. *Mylos'* twin building, a few blocks away by the port, I noticed, looked lonely and desperate for fixing.

"What do you want, Troy?" I shouted back.

"Your mom is here. Come for breakfast. The door is open."

She did not have to tell me twice. I was starving. I exited Mom's apartment through the kitchen door and started climbing down the small cemented and round staircase, thinking about the two *Myloi* (one by the park and one by the port). They were built in the early 1920s to be used as wheat warehouses. The trains would come and pick up the wheat to carry it to Piraeus. Both buildings served as German headquarters during WWII. On their roofs there used to be a siren to warn citizens of airplane raids and an anti-aircraft canon. Many times, with my brother and other neighborhood kids, we played through the rubble of each level of the *Mylos* by the park, not understanding the clear dangers hidden by broken window glasses and missing steps in wooden ladders connecting the floors.

I forgot how tough it was to climb down this emergency staircase. I gripped the iron railing to help make it safely to the ground. I turned left, and left again, to walk to the front of the apartment building. A hefty pavement of several meters separated the building from Psaron Street. Since the construction of Mom's house, Uncle had planted fruit trees in four equidistant spots he had selected at the end of the pavement and near the edge of the street. A few years back, as one fruit tree died, he planted an olive tree that with its fullness and fast growth, eventually became Uncle's pride. I could not help noticing that there was no olive tree in the pavement any longer and its spot remained empty.

I did not need to ring Auntie's doorbell, which was located to the right of the address sign, 'Psaron 110' and to the left of the main glass door with its grey metallic frame. The door was open. But before I entered, I glanced quickly to my immediate right at the old cottage that was an eyesore: unoccupied and in bad structural condition. That's where Persari died, I thought. Attached to this cottage was my late aunt Kaliopi's taverna. It had been changed to a two-room rental by her daughter, and my cousin, Katerina. Behind the taverna, Aunt Kaliopi's old house was left unchanged and in much need of a rebuild.

Instead of the elevator, I took the marble stairs to the fifth floor to exercise my legs. Troy was waiting for me outside the door. She gave me a hug and was going to give me a kiss but I stopped her.

"Troy, please don't kiss me when you have been smoking," I said, grimacing.

"Okay. Okay. I will go and brush my teeth and then chew gum. Come in. We are waiting for you," she said, taking my hand and pulling me into the living room.

Everybody was seated around the large table in the middle of the room drinking coffee: Mom, Auntie, Soula, and *Papou* (grandfather) Panagiotis, Auntie's father. Soula and *Papou* got up and gave me a hug followed by a kiss on each cheek. Breakfast was ready for me: scrambled eggs with fries, Greek salad with no onions, and toasted bread, all served by Soula. Troy came back after brushing her teeth and chewing gum. She kissed me lightly on the cheeks, explaining my previous complaint to a puzzled Soula. Over the course of my meal, I had to go over my marital situation for everyone to hear. Mom already had a chat with them about my marriage but they wanted to hear it from me one more time.

"I just don't understand," *Papou* said. "I loved Klaritsa when you brought her here in 1991. She was so sweet. And my wife, who is dead now, God bless her crazy soul, liked her a lot. What happened?"

"Jealousy!" Troy answered.

"I am not jealous of Stavros," Soula intervened like someone had accused her. "I am telling him all the time. You want to go with another woman? Go for it. Have your dinner. But you need to come back to me for the dessert. And if you bring a disease with you, I am going to CUT IT OFF." Everybody laughed except me.

"Stavros will never do this," *Papou* said. "Good men don't do this."

"Oh yeah? Look who is talking. What about your girlfriend?" Soula countered. She turned toward me.

"He has a girlfriend for a few years now. She is twenty years younger. People say she is taking his retirement money for letting him touch her breasts," she said jokingly.

"She has no need for money. Uncle Panagiotis still 'has it' and he is very 'operational'. Right, Uncle?" Troy said from behind the kitchen island as she put the dishes away.

Uncle claimed that his father-in-law, Panagiotis, had always had girlfriends. Panagiotis's wife, Stavroula, was a couple of years older than him, a major negative to the marriage. She was walking with a limp and no villager wanted to marry her. Panagiotis, a handsome young man, grabbed the opportunity and got her father's blessing along with a nice dowry for her. His life with her afterwards took him through some steep curves although they remained together until she passed away.

For instance, he would walk for many hours to take his cows from Kastania down to Kalamata to sell them. When he returned to the village the day after, Stavroula would accuse him of going with other women. In his anger, he would get the wooden Pizza peel from the made-of-bricks wood-fired oven, and slap her buttocks. Stavroula, in retaliation, would not allow him to see his daughter, using the strategy of putting the child to sleep early before Panagiotis returned from farming late in the afternoon.

"He had sex with her only once," Uncle would tell me teasingly. "After that, she did not let him touch her again because when he took her virginity she was in so much pain. But, one time was enough for your aunt to be conceived. Stavroula would sleep with your aunt all the time and Panagiotis would not dare do anything. But there were plenty lonely widows after WWII in the village and in need of a man." However, that was stretching the truth. Panagiotis did have sex with Stavroula a few times, although it may not have been consensual. She had three miscarriages before her only daughter, Eleni, was born.

"What am I supposed to do? I am a man you know!" *Papou* said apologetically.

"Is Ourania coming to the funeral? If she is, she needs to behave," Auntie said, slowly massaging her forehead with her hands. It looked like she was fighting a headache.

"She is coming and she told me she is also coming here today or tomorrow to see how you are doing," *Papou* answered, much to the disapproval of Auntie.

Eleni and Soula started cleaning the table. Mom left to go rest because later in the afternoon people would arrive to offer their sympathies. I decided to take a drive to check on the seafront. From the port, only a couple of minutes away from the neighborhood, I followed the road along the coastline passing the many restaurants and cafeterias, all largely empty as most Greeks rest in the early afternoon. I ended up driving on a narrow road climbing the mountain

Taygetos. The road led me to the bar Kastraki (*Little Castle*). Located halfway up the mountainside and overlooking the Messinian Gulf, the bar's location allows a guest to have a wonderful view of the city. The décor emphasizes a Middle Ages' theme with a knight's armor statue waiting to greet guests just before the semicircular stony entry. I parked the car and enter the covered area. The uncovered area was closed for the winter. There were only two couples seated by the large windows, drinking their beverages and enjoying the view. I sat by the bar and asked the female bartender for a cold milky frappé.

"Nice day, right?" she said as she left the foamy coffee in front of me.

"Yes. Really nice day. The sun is magnetizing the sea. The water is so calm for November," I replied, looking through the windows and letting my gaze fill the void inside me.

"Magnetizing the sea. Wow! That's something that I do not hear very often. We did not have such nice weather this week. We were closed until yesterday because it was a little stormy here in the mountain. We opened last night and, of course, today. Are you from around here?"

Clearly, she wanted to make conversation. After all, that's a bartender's job, isn't it? To open you up, listen to your worries, and provide you with an opportunity to express your feelings without you being afraid of any repercussions.

"I was born here," I told her. "In fact, I was born in the town's hospital that was destroyed in the 1987 earthquake."

"Oh my God! The big earthquake? Were you here then? I was a child at the time and I still remember it."

"I was here for holidays in the summer of 1987," I recalled. "But then I left at the end of August. The earthquake, I believe, hit the city in September sometime. I don't remember the exact date."

"The new ferry line, Kalamata-Crete, was opening that afternoon," she told me. "Most people were by the port to observe the mayor's proceedings. And then, we thought that the rumbling was the ferry's engines. I was on my dad's shoulders. I saw a huge mushroom cloud, full of dirt, rising from the city's Centre. Soon after that everyone went crazy. People were screaming and crying and running around. It was chaos."

I knew all about the 7.0 earthquake that hit Kalamata and its surrounding areas in 1987. Quite a few old villages were left in rubble and nearly sixty percent of the city was destroyed. The quake was funny, according to observers. Houses on one side of a street were levelled while others across the street were left standing. Mom's and Auntie's houses were damaged but not to the point that they had to be demolished like a few of the other houses down the block.

Aunt Kaliopi told me that Uncle's apartment building was swinging back and forth, bending like a stick. She would recall: "Stavroula was on the fifth floor's balcony and she was screaming for help. People on the street were telling her to go inside and hide under a bed but she was holding onto the railing for dear life, screaming. When the first shake stopped a brave man run upstairs to get her. He had to fight her to get her to let go of the rail."

"We raised money in Canada to help the folks here," I said.

"Thank you. What a nightmare. A lot of people were in tents for a few months. But the good thing was that the old buildings were destroyed and new buildings took their place. That boosted the economy as everybody had a job. Not like now where we are struggling economically."

I took a sip. The coffee tasted great. She looked satisfied, watching me clean the foam from my lips with the paper napkin.

"Do you like your coffee?"

"Yes. Very much, but I have to drink it fast because I need to get back to my aunt's house. You see, my uncle passed away and we have visitors coming."

"What's your uncle's name?"

"George. George Thimouleas."

"Thimouleas of the Gateas clan?"

My great grandfather, George Thimouleas, was a lighthouse keeper in the small town of Karthamyli. His job was not only to keep the oil burning and the reflective shield spinning around the flame but also to take his binoculars and search the sea for hours long. The locals kept saying that he looked like a 'gatos' (γατος - male cat). Eventually, the nickname Gateas stuck to him (and his wife became Gatina [female cat]), and it clung to the Thimouleas' generations that followed. Villagers with the same last name had other nicknames to allow differentiation.

"Yes, Thimouleas of the Gateas clan," I nodded.

"I know of you," she said with excitement.

I scanned her face, covered in part by her long, brown, curly hair. No clues there or in her big brown eyes. Behind her, the large bar mirror revealed a well-formed body. She wore tight jeans. A white V-cut t-shirt allowed a red butterfly tattoo on her upper back and between her shoulder blades to show. Before I tried to ask her who she was, she answered like she understood the question coming.

"I am Eleni. Your aunt's cousin. She told us that you were coming with your mom from Canada. Leonarthos, right? I heard so many nice things about you."

I didn't know what to say other than, "Oh, I see!"

In the conversation that followed, she told me she had seen photos of me at Auntie's house and that Uncle was so proud of me. She recalled Uncle bragging that I was a Principal in Vancouver, as well as, a professor at the University of Phoenix, an American University. Before I left, I nicknamed her Kastraki to remember where I met her.

Back in Auntie's house, Troy and Soula could not believe that I had met one of their younger cousins, Eleni. They were not sure if she was coming to the funeral but they were going to call her father once again to confirm his family's attendance.

"She is beautiful. Isn't she?" Troy muttered.

"She sure is," I said.

"Stay away from her. You are MINE."

"Oh Troy. Whatever you say," I teased her.

In less than half an hour, Auntie's two-bedroom apartment was full of visitors, mostly women from her work. They were seated either in the living room, the balcony or the kitchen. Mom's childhood friend also came to give her condolences, Mrs. Voula Kalampoki. My brother and her older son Taki were schoolmates. Her younger son Vassilis, was a year younger than me.

Takis first, and Vassilis, a couple of years later, moved to United States to complete their studies. Many years later, I did get in touch with Takis through Facebook. He was in Florida, married with children and working in his father-in-law's restaurant. Vassilis finished his PhD and he also got married. They both had no plans to return to Greece. Yet, they pushed their widowed mother to offer her large property 'in consideration' for an apartment building.

"Leonarthe mou. I am so glad you brought your mother home. How are you?" Mrs. Voula said when she saw me. She gave me a hug and kissed my cheeks.

"She would have come anyway, Mrs. Voula, without me. There was no way that we could have kept her in Vancouver when her beloved brother passed away. I am doing okay under the circumstances. But it feels like a dream."

"If you need any help at all just let me know. And you better bring her to visit me. You know where I live, right?"

"I think I do. I think your *polikatikia* is in the corner of Thoukithithou Street and Nethontos Street."

"That's right. I live on the fourth floor. Call me first before you guys come. Your mother has my phone."

"Do you remember the orange and mandarin trees in her farmhouse?" Mom asked. "You kids used to cut them and eat them. And you were playing soccer around the trees all the time."

"Are you hungry, my love?" Troy interrupted the conversation.

She was holding a platter with small food bites and cut fruit. I did not bother to try anything. To my question about where my aunt and *Papou* were, Troy answered that Auntie was resting and *Papou* went to the park's restaurant to see his friends.

I excused myself from Mom, Troy, and Mrs. Voula, but not before Mom reminded me that tomorrow was Monday and I had to go to Athens to pick up my sister Angela from the airport. On my way out of the apartment, Soula told me my childhood friend Sotiria was visiting with her older daughter Garyfalia and was asking where I was. In Mom's house, I enjoyed the quietness of the place. As I lay on the bed I thought that the day had gone by very fast. It did not take me long to fall asleep.

The Family Tree

In 1917, the two mothers, Kaliopi Thimouleas, nicknamed Gatina, and Maria Levi, agreed to have their children married. Kaliopi had eight daughters but one of them, Katerina, in her mid-twenties, was unmarried. Maria Levi had an unmarried son in his late forties, Ioannis (Yannis), who was in America. A perfect arrangement it seemed. Yannis came to Greece and after a two-year marriage he left again for America, leaving Katerina behind with a baby girl and pregnant again. He stayed for five more years in the foreign lands, working hard, and sending money back home to Katerina.

Katerina Thimouleas was able to save the money sent by her husband and buy a property for one hundred thousand drachmas across from the train station, not far from Kalamata's port. A few family members tried to change her mind that it was a bad investment but to no avail. She closed the deal, buying two small houses with a garden and a couple of cottages. She signed the official transfer paper by putting her thumb in the black ink and pressing it against the page. One cottage was rented for extra income and the other, used as a taverna. There was a courtyard connecting all the buildings with a small laundry-washroom room at its very centre. The washroom had no toilet seat. Instead, a hole in the ground was serving its purpose and was used pretty much by everyone, including the taverna's customers.

Katerina, although not educated, used her life smarts to operate the businesses. For instance, when she was running the taverna, she used small rocks to count how many beverages a person consumed. At times, she would buy a patron a drink with the proviso that he would pay attention and count how many beverages others were consuming.

In 1921, the city wanted to buy Katerina's houses for one hundred and fifty thousand drachmas to build a *Mylos*. She refused, believing that the train station and the *Mylos*' workers (if and when it was built) would benefit her businesses. She was right. When her husband came back, he found his wife operating a small estate. However, to maintain his role as the head of the family, he decided to get a good paying job shoveling coal in the local ferry's engine boiler.

Katerina and Yannis Thimouleas, of the Gateas clan, did not agree much on anything. All the property was in Katerina's name and she refused to put Yannis's name on it. To complicate things further, Yannis's mother reminded him at every instant that he was 'the man' and the house needed to be in his name. Nevertheless, Katerina's argument was that her husband was wasteful and not business-like—often wanting to give money to his relatives. In addition, he would spend money to buy food for their kids unnecessarily, as far as she was concerned. "If you don't eat breakfast for a few days then you stop being hungry in the morning," Katerina used to say to her daughters but she would gladly feed her only son breakfast.

The Thimouleas had four children. The first one, Afroula, was born in 1920 and not named after Yannis's mother because Katerina was not fond of her. The next two children, Kaliopi, born in 1927 and George (Yiorgos), born in 1930, were named after Yannis's mother and father respectively. When Katerina became pregnant for the fourth time, she thought it would be a boy she could name Michalis, after her father. Unfortunately, the child, born in 1933, was a female so she named her Maria, after her mother.

As Europe was about to embark in another dark chapter of its history, Afroula, at age sixteen, fell in love with a young man of the same age named Kiriako Koutava, born in Romania but of Greek descent, and working in the port's excavator ship. A couple of years later, she accidentally became pregnant. In July 1,1939, two months before the start of WWII, they got married and moved to Athens. They had two daughters and a son: Eleni, Kaiti, and Kostantinos.

Kaliopi fell in love at age seventeen with a *Mylos* (by the port) worker named George Kalouthis, born in the island of Samos. He was twenty. A couple of years later and in the global mist following the end of WWII, they got married. Kaliopi had a miscarriage that apparently was a boy, and then three daughters: Vassiliki (Vasso), Katerina (Kaiti), and Aggeliki (Aggelo). Kaliopi got one of her mother's cottages as a dowry and she was allowed to operate the taverna for 100 drachmas rent per month. Kaliopi and George extended the cottage behind the taverna, adding a couple of rooms for the girls.

In 1946, Thimouleas's only son George, received his engineering diploma from the Royal Navy Academy in Nastathmos, a naval academy by Athens, and started sailing with the Greek merchant ships. His dream was to go to America and make money. He was partly successful as he lived in America for a few years. He met a young woman called Margarita and they fell in love. However, her father, who owned a restaurant, did not give his consent for the wedding. George, heartbroken, left America for Greece. Margarita, equally heartbroken, never got married.

George would often embark as an engineer on the Greek merchant ships. At age forty-two, he decided to stop wandering the continents and stayed in Kalamata. He found a job as a mechanic at Karelia Tobacco Company (KTC). As a bachelor, he was picky. His ideal woman would have a nice body, young, blonde, a virgin, and be educated with at least a secondary school diploma. Four years later, he married by arrangement Eleni, from the village of Kastania. She worked in the main offices of KTC. She was a little bit overweight for George's liking, but she was sixteen years younger, blonde, virgin, and a high school graduate. They had no children.

Maria Thimouleas was the only child of Katerina and Yanni Thimouleas who continued with her schooling as she was determined to become a Physical Education teacher. Her father passed away (age undetermined) from prostate cancer in 1951 when Maria was 18 years old and in her last year of high school. On the day he passed away, she had come home from school to find him in bed where he had been laying the last couple of months. She had bought some 'karameles' for him to chew. She acted like she was angry.

"You said that your brother will pay for me to go to university in America. Why don't you pay for me?"

He coughed. Then he gave her a smile. The prostate cancer made him a ghost of his old self.

"You were my little baby and when you were hungry I would cook for you, much to the dismay of your crazy mother," he whispered. "I took care of you because you were skinny and weak and it was breaking my heart to see you go hungry. Your mother would only spend money for your brother, Yiorgo. I remember your sister, Kaliopi, cheating your brother to steal his food because she was so hungry. You see, during WWII, there was not much food around."

"I remember," Maria said. "*Mana* would let me sleep with her because it was so cold and I was freezing. And the roof was leaking so she had a bucket by her bed. And you were sleeping on the couch. She did not let you sleep with her."

He held her hand. His voice was very weak and scratchy. His smile left his face as his eyes closed. He whispered, "Maria mou. She used you for an excuse not to give me sex."

"She told us that you could not have any and that your balls were burnt because for so many years you were putting coal in the engines. But I did not mind sleeping with her because she would let me put my frozen feet between her legs to warm them up."

His hand relaxed. Maria kept holding it for a while and then she let go. With tears in her eyes, she screamed for her mother.

In 1955, George Thimouleas met Felix Hutchinson, who was the radio operator in the cargo ship 'Lemos'. One day over drinks in George's cabin, Felix noticed Katerina's and Maria's Thimouleas's black and white portrait. He fell irresistibly in love with Maria's facial characteristics, highlighted by the photographer's black pencil. Days later, after an early shift, George went to his cabin to find Felix daydreaming while holding the portrait. Felix admitted he was in love with Maria (or her photo). George was angry. He felt Felix's crush for his younger sister was inappropriate. However, eventually Felix gained George's trust and they became friends.

Felix learned to read and write in Greek using a

dictionary. Soon enough he was writing letters and sending American dollars as gifts to Maria, who had nothing to reply. Finally, she wrote a letter back to her brother. Among other things she quoted her mother. 'Yiorgo, who is this Barbarian bothering your sister? What does he want? Maria will not marry a foreigner.'

But George wrote back explaining Felix's good qualities and his trust toward him. His letter ended with three sentences: "He wants nothing. He would be a good husband for Maria. I am okay with him."

Katerina, as always, would listen to her son's wishes. She agreed that a man who does not ask for a dowry is a good man, even if he is a "Barbarian". After all, her son was "okay with him". Maria had no say. Her brother knew better.

Maria and Felix Hutchinson married in Venice on May 18, 1957 on the cargo ship 'Lemos'—that was the first time they actually saw each other in person. Hence, the joke to Maria from her children, "You were cheaper than a cow, Mom." But the joke was on them, as Maria was able, with her brother's help and her husband's money, to build in 1960 a two-levelled apartment building, with each level having three bedrooms. Later on, during the decade of the 1990s she added a two-bedroom penthouse with access to the kitchen, from the existing small circular staircase in the back of the building. That way, the apartment building would be distributed as an inheritance amongst her three children: Ioannis would get the ground level; Leonarthos, the second level; and Angela, the penthouse.

Katerina Thimouleas passed away in 1972 and in her will, left everything to her son, Yiorgo. That did not sit well with his two older sisters, Afroula and Kaliopi, who asked for part of their mother's estate. George kept half of the property for him and divided the remaining property between his sisters.

But none of them was satisfied. Furthermore, they could not come to an agreement to combine their assets and build something better. Neither could their children.

Finally, George, along with his wife and parents in-law, built his own apartment building attached to Maria's building. Literally! The first level was used for his business, making fireplaces and solar heating panels of his own invention. The second and third levels, mostly unfinished, were full of useless stuff—not according to him but according to his wife. The fourth and fifth floors were finished and furnished. George, Eleni, and her parents lived on the fifth floor while the fourth floor was mostly used to host visitors.

Episode 6

Sister's Arrival

I woke up with the sound of church bells. I got dressed and smelled the aroma of brewed coffee. I took a look at the kitchen before I entered the bathroom. Mom was not there. I completed my morning routine — brushed my teeth, shaved the slight hair growth, wet and combed my hair, added a couple of 'Eternity For Men' drops below my ears and headed to the balcony. Mom, Troy, and Soula were having coffee. An extra coffee cup was also waiting for me on the table. The birds' socialization across the street was interrupted by Troy's comment.

"I was going to wake you up with kisses!"

"Leave him alone," Soula added. "He is tired."

"Leonarthe. You need to wake up and go to Athens to pick up your sister," I heard Mom's sharp voice and a nudge to my left knee interrupted my dream.

"Should I wake him up with kisses?" Troy's voice sounded playful.

"Leave him alone. He is tired," Soula said.

I opened my eyes with my confusion triggering anxiety.

My mom was by the end of the bed while Troy and Soula peeked from the doorway, checking me out. That's weird, I thought. Did what I dreamt just happen?

"Ela," Mom said, this time with a softer voice. "Wake up. It is nine o'clock already. I have coffee ready."

She left the room, following the other two, who were laughing on the balcony. After I finished getting ready I joined them for a coffee. The plan, according to Mom, was simple: "Leave early because your sister arrives at two in the afternoon with Lufthansa. It's better to wait than be late."

Half an hour later, I was leaving Kalamata. The new highway, built in the last few years with European Community transfer money, cut through the mountains and made the trip to Athens an enjoyable one. I did not mind that every few kilometers I had to stop for a moment to pay the tolls. The employees at the booths were all very pleasant, willing to exchange a smile and wish me a good trip. In comparison, the old highway had no tolls but its many curves, going up and down the mountains, created a driving nightmare, especially when drivers got stuck behind a bus or a track.

I pushed the rental car to its limit, driving to speeds reaching from 140 to 160 kms at times. With only one short stop at Goody's fast food restaurant to have a snack and fill up the gas tank, I made the trip to Athens in about three-and-a-half hours, reaching the airport before 2:00 pm.

Angela looked tired but overall was feeling alright. She had a very busy past few days trying to find a locum to substitute for her at the North Road Medical Clinic where she was a doctor. During the trip back to Kalamata, I filled her in on what had transpired since Mom and I had arrived in Athens. She was mainly concerned about Auntie's and Mom's frame of mind. She brought with her sedatives and other medication that could help the two women withstand the ordeal of the funeral of a loved person.

I called Mom when I was in the town of Messini to inform her that we were twenty minutes away from home. She told me to go to Auntie's apartment where everyone was waiting for us.

I parked the car in one of the very few street spots left. As the rather cool night was settling early, the Kalamata Municipal Railway Park was busy with kids playing in the trains and adults watching a soccer game in the restaurant's outside screen display. I left my sister to take the elevator to the fifth floor while I carried her suitcase to the penthouse.

As I headed towards Auntie's apartment I saw many of her relatives, visiting from her village of Kastania, getting into their cars. I recognized a few of them but did not bother to engage. In the apartment, Soula was tidying up the place with the help of Sofia, her mother in-law, and my sister. I took a moment to say hello to Papou, Auntie, and Mom, who were seated at the kitchen table all quiet. I spotted Stavros on the balcony smoking a cigarette and I headed toward him.

"Hi Stavro," I said, shaking his hand. "What's going on with the funeral arrangements?"

"We have good and bad news, Leonarthe. The good news is that there was a cancelation so everything is going to take place tomorrow. The church proceedings and the cemetery to put Uncle to rest are all arranged. The bad news is that your aunt wanted to go to our cousin Peris' small restaurant but we have invited about sixty people and that's too many. So, I booked the cemetery restaurant for coffee and dessert."

"Okay. So what's the program then?"

"You and the women need to be in Ekklisia (church) Analipsi at eleven-thirty in the morning. The men from the funeral home will be there to set up the flowers outside and inside the church. The hearse will arrive around noon. The service should not take more than half an hour; then we will go to the nekrotafio (cemetery) in Ekklisia of Agios (Saint) Charalampos. After we put Uncle in the ground we will have coffee and cake in the small restaurant by the Square Nekrotafiou. It's near the small shopping mall called Aithrio. Eleni, my sister, will show you. We should be done by five-ish in the afternoon. Later on, we may have dinner for the family only. We will see."

"Wow, that's a full day," I remarked. "Good on you for arranging all these in such a short time, Stavro. Could I ask you, what's the cost?"

"I didn't ask the funeral home for costs because your aunt doesn't care. If I will start talking to her about costs she'll take my head off."

I agreed with him. Auntie wanted to have the best funeral arrangements possible for the only man she had ever loved. And she was not poor either. I went to find my sister and talk to her about tomorrow's program. She told me that she gave a sedative to Auntie but Mom did not want any. We agreed that she would stay with Auntie and Mom during the proceedings so that I could take pictures and video clips of the service in the church and the cemetery. I asked her if she wanted to go and visit Sotiria, our childhood friend. She refused, claiming that she was too tired and she was ready to go to sleep. She and Mom left soon after.

Troy and I decided to visit Sotiria although it was getting late in the evening. We walked the sort distance to Sotiria's apartment on the poorly lit street, in about five minutes. During that time, I explained to her that Sotiria's family and my family had established a close relationship being neighbors for many years. My sister and Sotiria were of the same age and playmates. Every day they would walk together to the 8th Elementary School, mostly accompanied by Sotiria's mother, up and until the end of Grade Six. That was when Mom moved us to Oinoussai Island, the 'Heavenly Island', as we would call it at times.

Mr. Nikos and Mrs. Roubini Sofronas were not able to have a child. In 1965, they adopted a baby girl and named her Sotiria (Ritsa), meaning salvation. Nikos was a beacon in the Ekklisia Ipapantis by the feet of the Kalamata Acropolis, where the city's Castle was located. He passed away in December 12, 1989 when Sotiria was twenty- four- years old. Mrs. Roubini, with her husband's small pension, kept her house located behind Thimouleas's property, in good standing. She lived to see her daughter get married to Aris Karyotas in the Spring of 1990 but died only a few months later, on August 22, 1990.

Aris and Ritsa Karyotas had two daughters. Garyfalia, named after Aris's mother, and Niki, who was named after Ritsa's father. Ritsa gave her parents' old property 'in consideration' to a construction company that built a five-levelled apartment building. The Karyotas received in return the apartments on the fourth and fifth floors to call their own.

Later on, they borrowed money from the bank and built a house by the feet of Taygetos Mountain, overlooking the Messinian Gulf. They used the natural red stones found all over in that area and Aris never shied away from describing the history and the natural wonders of the Mountain.

"According to Greek Mythology, the name, Taygetos came after 'Taygeti', the name of Pleionis's and Atlanta's daughter" Aris would declare. "Taygetos Mountain is the highest mountain range of the Peloponnese, located between the three areas of Arcadia, Laconia, and Messinia. The top of the mountain, called 'Profitis Ilias' (Prophet Elias), is 2.407 meters above sea level with a chapel named after the Prophet, generously offering to a spectator a breathtaking view of Peloponnese.

The Byzantines called the mountain 'Pendathaktylos', or 'five fingers'. That is, because there are five tops on the mountain range. With two rivers, Evrotas and Nethodas, which drain into the Laconian and Messinian Gulfs respectively, the mountain provides plenty of hiking routes that are well signposted and attract a lot of travelers during the summer period."

Unfortunately, the location of the house, surrounded by nature's beauty, did not help the Karyotas in selling it to at least recover the borrowed money. The Greek economy collapsed, leaving them in despair and on the brink of bankruptcy. Yet, they somehow were able to economically survive and pay for their daughters' education. But the young women, with their degrees, did not help the family's financials much, as everyone in the family struggled to find a decent job.

Ritsa's apartment building's entrance was in Themistokleous Street, across from the ENA food department store located on the main floor of Mylos. As Troy and I entered the apartment on the fifth floor we got hugs and kisses from Garyfalia, Niki, and Ritsa, in that order. Ritsa's daughters did not look like her at all. Ritsa had a rather large body frame and she was quite tall. Both girls were good looking and had a slim body frame. Foivos, their black-and-brown colored Beagle rescue dog, growled persistently at us, indicating his displeasure. He had apparently been abused by humans and other dogs alike.

I met Foivos in my last visit to Greece and we did not hide our dislike of each other. On the island, I had three hunting dogs: Flora, Bella and Dick, and they were big dogs. In Canada, my dog, Ira, a lovely Lassie look-alike but with black and white fur, was trained by me not only to be my kids' protector but also a great companion. So, to my view, I knew how to deal with dogs' behavioral issues.

"Get lost buddy," I said sharply to Foivos. "If we will go to battle you will lose." Troy hid behind me, holding my hand, terrified.

Foivos barked and growled at me, showing his teeth and telling me to take back what I said. He looked ready to draw his 'guns'.

"FOIVOS BE QUIET," Ritsa shouted. Garyfalia picked him up and put him on the balcony, closing the door behind him. He pressed his nose on the door glass with his large big eyes looking weird and evil in the reflective light.

"He does not like you," Troy said, still not letting my hand go.

"Oh, forget about him. He was abused and we are working on his behavior," Ritsa said apologetically. "Please sit down. Would you like some coffee?"

We refused but we did ask for a couple of glasses of water instead.

"Niki, bring them water," Ritsa ordered. "Where is Angela? Why didn't she come?" she asked me.

"She was very tired and wanted to sleep, considering that tomorrow is the funeral," I responded. "We are not going to stay long either. I am exhausted."

We did stay for about one hour, discussing mostly politics and the country's financial issues. It was close to eleven when Troy and I left the apartment and got into the elevator. She held my hand. I pressed the button to get us to the ground floor. I turned around to face her. In the white, dimly lit elevator light I spotted a single long, blonde hair grudgingly holding onto her T-shirt close to her neck. I raised my free hand to remove it. She grabbed my hand and, in one move, forced our joined hands around and behind my waist. Her lips locked with mine firmly. It was sudden and her kiss took me by surprise. Yet, somehow, my body language must have triggered the response.

"I wanted to kiss you since the hospital," she said, taking a breath.

"And now that you did, how was it?"

"Delicious. May I have another?" she sounded almost apologetic. She spread my legs apart by putting her leg between them. I let her pin me against the elevator's wall, holding her hands tight. Her lips were searching for mine. I laughed. I raised our locked hands between our chests, gently pushing her body away from mine a few centimeters. I kissed her softly on the cheek.

"There," I said. "Have another, silly. Come."

I led the way out of the elevator. We walked silently. The street seemed to be darker than before. The silence was not controversial or uncomfortable. Rather, it was controlled, begging for an understanding of what happened. Did emotions take over accidentally or was it an old rain check? Was it going to happen again? And if it was, who was going to write the 'How' and 'When', the 'If' and 'Then' statements? The minutes rolled by in slow motion. Eventually, we came around the block and to the pavement in front of Auntie's building. I broke the silence.

"Kalinixta (good night), Eleni."

She did not respond. Satisfied by her silence I started walking away. A few seconds later, she called my name. I turned to see her running toward me. She gave me a long bear hug and kissed my lips gently.

"Kalinixta, little Cousin," she said out of breath. "I love you. I always did!"

She turned around and walked away. I stood there watching her disappear behind the door. I turned right at the corner of Mom's building, and then right again to leave behind the streetlight's guidance. I started climbing the shadowy staircase leading to the penthouse, by gripping the iron railing.

"Crazy Troy!" I murmured, entering the penthouse's kitchen.

Episode 7

The Funeral

Stavros left early in the morning for the funeral home. We left *Pappou* Panagiotis at home. With Troy in the front seat of the rental car and Mom, Auntie, and Angela in the back seats, I arrived in the Ekklisia of Analipsi at 11:15 a.m. The bells were ringing harmonically. All four women were wearing black clothes with my sister and Mom also wearing black hats. I was wearing a black suit with a purple shirt, nicely ironed and prepped for the occasion by Troy. I parked the car in the large parking lot surrounding the church, in one of the spots reserved for 'family members', a few meters away from the church's front door.

The women stopped for a few minutes to join a couple of other people who were reading the ribbons in the many wreaths displayed just before the entrance. In one of them, the large white ribbon's text was reading: "To Our Brother, Uncle And Father. We Thank You! The Hutchinson Family." I snapped a photo of my family's wreath, recalling that we were all baptized in Ekklisia Analipsi: my brother Yanni by uncle George; me, by uncle, Kiriako Koutava; and my sister, by seventeen-year-old, Marigo Patitsas, the daughter of Captain Leon Lemos, the owner and CEO of Lemos Merchant Ships Inc., the company that Dad and uncle George worked for. In fact, Captain Leon's brother, Captain Michalis Lemos, was supposed to baptize my sister but he fell sick in London prior to the baptism taking place. Marigo was accompanying her father to witness the baptism at the time. Captain Leon then asked his young daughter to replace his brother and thus Marigo became Angela's godmother. Father Lembesis was the priest who did all three baptisms. He was the parishioner of the church almost until his death.

We entered the church one at a time. Mom put money in the collection box and she got a candle for each of us. We lit our candles and placed them safely in the *menalia*. We proceeded, like all Orthodox faithful, by making the sign of the cross with our right hand from right to left. Then we slightly kissed the icon of Jesus's Resurrection and Ascension before we passed the Royal Doors to enter the nave.

"Leo, are you going to sit with us or are you going to take pictures and video the liturgy?" my sister asked me, interrupting my thoughts.

"I will take photos. You sit with them," I said nodding towards Mom and Auntie who were walking toward the chairs arranged in two rows in the front of the nave and slightly to the left of the main altar.

"Do you think Auntie will survive the ordeal?"

"I think so," my sister said. "I gave her extra meds."

The second row of chairs was occupied by a couple of older women dressed in black and covering their head with a black *mandili* (scarf). I asked Troy if she knew the women.

"They are from the village. They are *mirologistries*. They

71

are getting paid to lead the mourning. I am going to sit with them and sing along," she whispered.

I tested out the video camera, taking in the spectacle of the church as my family found their seats. Everything in the church was as I remembered it from my childhood years and vivid memories started to flow through my mind.

Father Lembesis would often hold services for the whole 8th Elementary School that belonged to his parish to celebrate special religious events. Father had the girls occupying the left side and the boys, the right side of the church, as was customary. I thought, at the time, that the right side symbolized 'manhood' while the left side was representing 'obeisance'.

In such events, some of my friends, forgetting why they were attending the services, would gesture to the girls across the nave. The girls would giggle silently with each other, bowing their heads, afraid of being seeing by their teacher Mrs. Aspacia, who normally accompanied them. I, on the other hand, preferred to go to the Chanter Spyros' altar and sign along with him the hymns. From that position, I could easily see what was going on between the boys and the girls. I also had a close view of Dina, whom I was in love with. She would be seated in the front row so that she could have a direct view of me as well.

After the conclusion of the services many children would stay for confession. Many times, I was the first one to confess my 'sins' as a privilege of helping with the chanting. Father Lembesis would ask the same six questions as a starter every time. "Did you steal anything? Did you lie to anyone? Did you swear? Did you have any impure thoughts? Did you obey your parents and your elders? Did you pray every night?" I would answer the first four questions with a "No, Father", and the last two with a "Yes, Father".

However, one time, he surprised me with the following question.

"Did you raise the skirt of a girl to check what is underneath it?" he asked, combing his white beard with his right hand's fingers.

"No, Father. I know what is under a girl's skirt," I answered

calmly.

"Oh, Yes? And what's that?"

"Her panties!"

"Don't you want to see a girl's panties?" he asked again, focusing his eyes sternly into mine from below his bushy eyebrows. His glasses hung desperately at the very edge of his nose.

"No," I replied with confidence. "It's a sin!"

He was satisfied with my answer but, of course, I was not telling the whole truth. Simply, I could not see a difference between a girl's panties and a girl's swimsuit. And during the summertime, I could watch hundreds of girls' swimsuits on the beach without having to lift any skirts.

When my confession was done, Father Lembesis would do his prayer, watching me make the sign of the cross properly. I moved my right hand from right to left, holding my thumb and first two fingertips pressed together, and the last two fingers pressed down to my palm. He was very particular when all the faithful performed the sign of the cross, as this reinforces the Orthodox faith in the Trinity (symbolized by the first three fingers pressed together) and the two natures of Christ as both God and Man (symbolized by the other two fingers). Finally, Father Lembesis would let me kiss the cross around his neck and the back of his right hand, in that order, before calling the next terrified child in the confession booth.

Dina's worry during my confession was that telling the truth would destroy our relationship. Father was known to visit parents and tell them what children had confessed to him. And that's why she never went to confession; faking fainting spells every time her mother dared to suggest it. But between us, and after every time I went to confession, Dina would pose the question to me, "Will we end up in hell?"

"We are only ten years old and hell doesn't want us," I would laughingly answer, easing her worries. But really, why hell would care about two kids being in love and dreaming about holding each other's hand when no one is watching?

Through the camera's lens I saw Troy walking through the central isle. I turned the camera off as the priest came out of the altar slightly bowing to the right, to the center, and to the left of the nave. He looked quite young with his hair combed back finishing in a ponytail. His short black beard was clean and stylish. He came down the three lengthy marble stairs that run across the iconostasis and introduced himself to Mom, Auntie, and Sister. Mom told him something and they both looked in my direction. He waved at me. I bowed my head in acknowledgement. Then, I went out of the church to wait for the hearse's arrival.

The hearse arrived at noon. Along with five other men, Stavros carried the casket into the narthex. The priest came to meet them. He said a short prayer before going through the Royal Doors shaking his *thimiatro* (incense-holding golden-plated cup supported by three chains) to the left and to the right, letting small clouds of incense disappear into the open space of the church. The casket carriers followed behind him.

The *mirologistries* started their mourning as soon as the casket was placed in front of Mom, Auntie, and Sister, on top of a table covered with a white satin cloth. The funeral home's two employees opened the top of the casket. They used a long, white satin cloth to cover Uncle's main body and placed pink roses over the cloth atop his chest. Uncle's head, looking frozen and stony, rested on a white pillow.

Auntie Helen let a scream float amongst the mourners' song. She got up from her chair and kissed Uncle on the forehead. She kept repeating the same sentences, "Yiorgo mou, why did you leave me? What am I going to do now? Yiorgo mou, agape mou."

Angela held Auntie's hand. Mom remained silent, her head bowed and her eyes closed. I resumed videotaping and taking pictures with my digital camera. Auntie bent over Uncle's face and asked me to take a photograph. That I did, capturing her sad look and the dark circles under her eyes. Her right cheek touching his forehead with her lips milliseconds away from kissing him; while her right hand rested slightly over his left lobe. Behind Auntie, the *mirologistria's* shadowy and deathly looking face was also captured in the dark top right hand corner of the photo.

"Please do not video or take photographs during the liturgy," the priest said, touching my shoulder. "The faithful shall get angry. The soul of the dead shall not find peace trapped in this world."

"Father, we live in the twentieth century. Please, do not say such things to me," I answered gently.

"If you are an Orthodox faithful you will understand and respect my wishes," he replied.

"Father, I was baptized in this church. So, I am an Orthodox. I do not consider myself religious so I may not be a perfect 'faithful' but I am extremely spiritual. I believe my uncle's memory will stay with me, photos or not. However, photos or videos don't capture souls. Having said this, it is your *Ekklisia* and I will respect your wishes."

He was satisfied, seeing me put the camera in my pocket. He started the liturgy. The *mirologistries* stopped mourning. I moved around the church, noticing Mrs. Toula Kalambokis and young Eleni from Kastraki. In one of the church's left side *stacidia*, I found my cousin, Aggeliki, daughter of my late aunt Kaliopi. When she saw me, she gave me a hug and shouted aloud, "Ah Thimoulea, why did you leave us?" A couple of women close by repeated her sentence.

"Are you okay?" I asked her. "You look pale."

"I feel I am going to faint," she said. "I need to get fresh air."

As soon as she finished the sentence her legs crumpled. I held her mid-section as she leaned on me for support. On our way out of the church through the eastern single side door, I grabbed a chair. Once outside, Aggeliki sat on the chair, taking deep breaths to replenish the missing oxygen from her lungs.

"Leonarthe, look," she said all of the sudden. "My freaking sister came to see what's going on."

"What do you mean? Where? Kaiti?" I asked her, looking around without expecting an answer.

"I just saw her driving by. She is not welcomed in this funeral after all the nasty things she has done to Thimoulea from taking him to the court for allegedly threatening her, to poisoning his beautiful olive tree in front of his house."

"How do you know that she poisoned the tree?"

"I know! Everyone knows! It was a BEAUTIFUL olive three."

"Well, if she decides to come we cannot really throw her out can we?"

"I will throw her out," Aggeliki said, taking a deep breath. "You know, she was supposedly taking care of my mother, your aunt, but she was really after her pension. And when my mother died she did not tell me anything. A neighbor was reading the paper's obituaries and asked me, 'Is your mother's last name Skoulikas?' Do you know why he said that? In the obituary she wrote, 'Kaliopi Skoulikas' instead of Kaliopi Kalouthi. Freaking Kaiti! Can you believe that? She did not use our family's last name but her husband's last name."

"LEOOOOO," the female shout came from the grey Mercedes car parked at Mpoumpoulinas Street. "LEOOOOO," she shouted again.

"Do you know her?" Aggeliki asked me, nodding

towards the blonde woman behind the wheel.

"I think I do," I said. "Give me a moment. I will be right back."

"Tell her to stop screaming. It is a funeral for God's sake."

I walked across the church's parking area feeling the sun-rays' disappearance. The weather was fast-changing with alarming moisture looming below some tender-looking clouds. Rain was coming!

"What a surprise Lita to see you in Kalamata," I said, lowering myself to rest my hands over the driver's side window.

"Oh my God, Leo! This is such a small world. After Patra, I decided to come to Kalamata with my girlfriends. We were driving around to find a taverna to get some lunch and we saw all the cars and the hearse. So, I said, 'Wow it's a funeral. Let's stop and watch. I have not seen a Greek funeral before.' And then you came out from that door. What a small world."

"A small world indeed, Lita. This is my uncle's funeral."

She ignored what I said, turning sideways to look at her female companions. "Girls, this is Leonardo," she said. "The guy I told you about. Leo, this is Nancy and Vicki. They are both American-Greek from Los Angeles."

I looked at the passenger's seat and then at the backseat. Nancy, the front passenger was a slightly overweight woman in her mid-twenties with rich, black straight hair. Vicki, probably of the same age, looked disinterested. She was attractive and busty. Her short, black curly hair covered much of her forehead. All of them wore mini-skirts and T-shirts, seemingly unaware of the change in the weather.

"You were right. He is cute," Nancy said in English. "Is he available?"

"He speaks English," Lita replied, also in English. "Careful what you say."

"Nice meeting you, ladies," I said in English. "And Nancy, no, I am not available. I am married with four kids."

"Oh stop it," Lita interrupted me, getting back into her Greek accent. "We are staying at Electra Hotel and Spa, a few blocks away from here, by the port. Promise me you will come for a visit."

"LEONARTHE," Troy's sharp and panicky voice reached me. I turned around to see her by the church's door, waving me to move towards her.

"I have to go. I'm sorry," I said apologetically, straightening up to move a step back away from the car.

"Promise," Lita begged. She reached through the window and grabbed my jacket.

"Okay, I will. Ciao." I said turning away, suddenly forcing her hand to free my jacket.

Troy looked upset. She did not see me for a little while in the church and she worried as the liturgy was about to end. I asked her if she saw my cousin, Aggeliki.

"Yes. Her son came and got her. She was not feeling well. She just left," Troy responded.

The services had just finished when we entered the church. The *mirologistries* were even louder now. I wasn't sure if they were repeating the same song or different ones. Auntie Helen looked weak and disoriented but from time to time she would let out a large cry, calling Uncle by his name. The medication that my sister gave her seemed to be working. For sure, everything was happening in a slow motion for her. Mom was quite drowned in her sadness. I joined them, offering my left hand to Mom for support as she got up from her seat.

The attendees formed a line and very quickly and

respectfully faced the altar, making the sign of the cross and paying their respects to me, Mom, Sister, Auntie and Uncle in that order. Some of them kissed his forehead while others touched the casket. The funeral home's employees asked us to go, much to the dismay of Auntie, who tried for a minute to defy them by leaning over and grabbing the casket, shouting Uncle's name. Angela pulled her back and whispered something in her ear. Auntie stopped shouting.

We led the way out of the church from the side door first; the same door that Aggeliki, Troy, and I used. Sister was holding Auntie and I was holding Mom. Suddenly, Mom cried, "Yiorgo mou, my brother and greatest supporter. You were like a father to my children."

Auntie followed Mom's cry with a scream, overpowering silent tears from many attendees and the *mirologistries* song. When out of the church, Stavros followed us to the car. "I will see you in the *nekrotafio* (cemetery)," he said to Troy and I. "Drive slowly as many cars will follow you."

The Cemetery of Saint Charalampos

Stavros was right. A few cars followed me to the cemetery of Saint Charalampos, North of the city's centre, a couple of blocks away from the monastery of St. Kostantinos. This is the monastery of the nuns who make the famous 'Kalamata satin handkerchiefs'. It took me twenty minutes of driving from the *Ekklisia* Analipsi to the Cemetery Square. I parked in one of the available spots and followed the women to the cemetery gates.

It started to drizzle. A small wind was getting braver and colder by the minute. We waited for the priest and the hearse by the cemetery's entrance, with the *mirologistries* right behind us, waiting like vultures for the dead body to arrive.

The hearse arrived half an hour later and the priest soon after. Stavros and his helpers, unloaded the casket. The priest led the way in one of the small paths between the many graves. He was followed by the men carrying the casket. We followed the casket: Auntie and Angela, Mom and

I, Troy and Soula. In sequence, we were followed by the *mirologistries*, who kept mourning, making the moist atmosphere weary of the death spread around. The rest of the attendees concluded the funeral line, many holding opened umbrellas.

We stopped by a freshly dug open grave. The fresh, wet soil piled up in the corner of the grave next to a marble stone lying on its side, waiting impatiently to relax on top of the casket. As people scrambled to find a spot between and around the many graves to watch the proceedings, Auntie's cry interrupted the priest's prayer.

"Yiorgo mou. Agape mou. Why did you leave me?"

Angela held Auntie tight and straight. The *mirologistries* lowered their voices, allowing the attendees to hear the prayer. Finally, the priest gave the go-ahead for the carriers to lower the casket down to fill the necessary gap. Mom was quiet, her head bowed. I could not tell if she was breathing but I was glad that the whole process was faster than I anticipated. Troy and Soula were sobbing. I decided not to take any photographs.

Peris, Auntie's cousin, who was one of the casket's carriers, put a small white plate on the marble stone.

"Who is going to break it?" he asked.

"Is he crazy?" a woman from the back of the line said. "This is bad luck."

"No, it's not," a man replied. "This is our custom in the village. The noise from breaking the plate allows the gates of the underworld to open."

"What underworld?" someone else said. "He is going to Heaven. Heaven is not in the underworld. Breaking the plate, it's a jinx."

"A jinx is what we think is a jinx. A custom is a custom," Peris intervened. "Father, what do you think it's best?"

"No one knows best," the priest said, making the sign of the cross. He took a fistful of soil and threw it on top of the casket. "Just let the dead rest in peace."

And with that, everyone seemed to get the point. The priest led the way back along the small path between the many graves. He was followed by Auntie and Angela, Mom and Soula, and a few of the attendees. Stavros, Troy and I, stayed behind to see the diggers cover the casket with the soil and to hear the *mirologistries* cry their last song.

Troy held my hand when she saw a couple of tears rolling down my cheeks. She rested her head on my shoulder. I did not bother telling her what I thought I saw. Surely, I was daydreaming seeing my Yiayia standing above Uncle's grave waving at me. I used to see her in my dreams for a few years after her death doing just that: waving at me!

Stavros asked me if I was doing alright. I assured him that I was fine, although I could feel a big knot in my stomach. I saw that the white plate was still on top of the marble stone. Stavros watched me stepping forcefully over it and breaking it into pieces. One of the four workers used his shovel to mix the broken pieces with the mud, before throwing them over the casket at the bottom of the grave.

Troy and I watched the workers covering the casket for a few more minutes before heading to the small restaurant by the Square Nekrotafiou. Mom, Angela, Auntie, and *Papou* Panagiotis were seated around a table near the restaurant's entrance, with glasses of water in front of them. Everyone else had already been served coffee and a piece of cake. People were socializing quietly, seated on available chairs or standing.

A woman, looking in her seventies and wearing a long black velvet coat came toward Troy and I, holding two cups of coffee.

"Thank you Ourania," Troy said, getting both cups. "I see you brought my uncle." She gave me one of the cups. "Leonarthe, this is Ourania," she announced, looking unhappy.

"You are Maria's son, right?" Ourania said, unleashing a stare that made me uncomfortable.

"Yes, I am. Why are you looking at me like that? Did I do something wrong?"

"No, you did not. Panagia mou, you are good looking. Φτου να μη σε ματιαξω," she said, following her sentence with spitting-like sounds as she clicked her tongue at the same time. Her words translated mean, 'I spit so that I don't give you the evil eye.' That is the way many Greeks have adopted to avoid giving the μάτι (*mati* - evil eye), to people or animals they admire, although the evil eye is also believed to be a curse cast by a malevolent glare, usually given to an unaware person.

The evil eye, known as μάτι (*mati*), 'eye', as an '*apotropaic*' visual device, is known to have been a fixture in Greece dating back to at least the 6th century BC. The *mati* is cast away through the process of *xematiasma* (ξεμάτιασμα) from a 'healer' or 'protector', who silently recites a secret prayer passed down from an older relative of the opposite sex, usually a parent or grandparent.

Mom was always my healer, as she learned from her grandmother the version of the prayer that takes the *mati's* energy away from the victim. When I would get sick with the *mati's* symptoms of nausea, yawning, and light headedness, she would perform the *xematiasma* to identify if I was indeed afflicted with the evil eye. If both Mom and I yawned profusely, then the verdict was that I was under a spell. That required Mom to perform the sign of the cross three times, and emit spitting-like sounds in the air three times.

In relation to this, one may accept Plutarch's explanation. He said that human eyes may be the sole source of possible deadly rays, like poisoned arrows, come out from the inner recesses of a person possessing the evil eye, to inflict misery upon a victim. Hence, I was thankful Ourania did her spitting, as I had been susceptible to the evil eye since I was a child.

I think I was six years old when I had nightmares that somehow would influence my spirituality. The nightmares were of two kinds. Ones that I would see myself falling off into a vacuum before a mountain's rocks crushed me leaving me breathless; and ones that would take me inside a dream of a dream, where something powerful was making me powerless and unable to move. I remember hiding my head under my pillow so that the nightmares would not get me and then waking up screaming for help.

Of course, Mom took me to the doctor but that did not accomplish much. And then one night, I recall lit candles around my bed and Persari and Yiayia praying, each holding a candle. Perhaps I was dreaming but there were other images circling around my bed as well. Ghosts? Spirits? Who knows! And then, cold drops of water were dropped on my head and Yiayia's words of prayer got louder. "Holy Virgin, Our Lady, if Leonarthos is suffering from the mati, release him of it." The words were repeated two more times before the candles light was eradicated.

I do not recall having those particular nightmares after that xematiasma. Yiayia much later explained to me that there are people who give the evil eye and people who take it. There is no neutrality. However, it is possible for someone to give the evil eye to him or herself. Yiayia thought that the worst negative energy is transmitted by a blonde, blue-eyed woman and I should be aware of that. Yet, any set of eyes could also inflict a devastating blow to me, if I was not careful.

I grew up getting the evil eye often and regularly, learning to identify the symptoms and seek help from Mom. She could even take the *mati* away by speaking to me on the phone. But, on Saturday August 15, 1987, Mom was not available, as I was in Kalamata and she was in Vancouver.

On that date, I met my childhood friend, Veni, in the cafeteria Athanasiou by the port. August 15, called Dekapentavgoustos (Δεκαπενταυγουστος), is a special day for the Greek Orthodox Church as faithful celebrate the Assumption of the Virgin Mary by God into Heaven. Veni and I, chose not to sit inside the air-conditioned restaurant but to cross Navarinou Street and sit in one of the tables covered by large umbrellas. The sun's heat was radiating a healthy 40 plus degrees Celcius.

I had not seen Veni for many years and visiting Kalamata for the first time after my family's departure to Canada in 1979, I made it my priority to meet up with him. We were enjoying talking about everything and anything while drinking our cold frappe the server brought us. Suddenly, fear surrounded me that someone was looking at me. I turned to see a tall blonde woman wearing black clothes. She was standing across the street by the cafeteria's wide-open doors staring at my direction.

"Veni, do you know her?" I whispered to my friend, lowering my eyes careful not to look at her.

"Who?" he replied.

"The blonde woman by the door. She is staring at us."

He turned around. He took a few seconds before he responded.

"Where? There is nobody there."

Indeed, there was no one by the cafeteria's front door. Somehow I was relieved. Then, my stomach started to get upset. Was it the coffee? I was feeling sick. Was it the heat? My face was getting numb. Veni noticed the drastic physical changes and the sweat dripping down on my face.

"Are you okay?" he asked.

"I don't know," I answered. "I feel sick, like I need to throw up."

"Your face is gone white, Loni," he said using my nickname. "Could it be the sun?"

"I am not sure. I think I may have the mati."

"Oh shit," Veni said standing up right away. "Oh shit. Let's go. I know an old woman who can help you."

He drove like a maniac to the east side of town, occasionally pushing my head back on my seat, as I fought to stay conscious. We reached a small square surrounded by old houses and a few small trees that were begging for water. As soon as he parked his car, the front door of a rundown brick house opened. The old woman who came out was shouting and pulling her white hair.

"BRING HIM IN. BRING HIM IN. HURRY, THE MATI WAS STRONG."

Veni helped me out of the car. Once inside her house, the smell of incense and the darkness of the place lit with candles overpowered me. A large wooden cross depicting Jesus's crucifixion was hanging by a nail on the wall. Veni put me down on the only available couch and rested my head on a pillow.

"He is bad. Isn't he?" I heard him saying.

"She was blonde. Blue-eyed blonde," she said pushing a little table closer to me. "I knew you men were coming. I could feel you were coming. She drank his energy."

The old woman placed one drop of olive oil in a glass of water. The drop sank to the bottom of the glass, to Veni's disbelief. Two more drops she added. They merged. The merging of the drops meant that someone tried to draw out and consume my energy. The old woman sighted in disbelief. She dropped more olive oil drops in the water. Nine in total! They all merged and in a matter of a minute or so they dissolved in the water, Veni told me later on.

She started saying a prayer and making the sign of the cross from *time to time while Veni watched over me. She asked him to raise my head. As he did she brought the glass to my lips.*

"DRINK THE WATER," she ordered. "Drink in the name of the Father and the Son and the Holy Spirit. Her black clothing shall disappear. Her heart shall be erased. Her eyes shall be punished."

I drank a little bit of the water slowly. She dipped her thumb in the water and pressed it against my forehead, making the sign of a cross three times. Veni allowed my head to rest back on the pillow.

"Thank you, Yiayia," I heard him saying. "Can I help you with some money to buy candles in the church?"

"No, it is alright. She was blonde. Blue-eyed blonde," she said putting her hand on my chest. "Let him rest. Come back to get him in an hour or so."

One month later, when I was back in Vancouver, Veni informed me that the old woman had passed away in her sleep.

Troy's voice brought me back to the restaurant's noise and away from my thoughts.

"What are you thinking?" she said. "You look concerned about something."

"Nothing much," I lied convincingly while turning toward Ourania.

"Thank you for the compliment, Ourania," I said with a smile. "Much appreciated. I am going to sit with my family now."

I left Troy and Ourania and I sat on a chair at the table where the family was seating. Stavros came along and whispered something to Auntie. She nodded her head up and down like she was okay with what he was proposing. Then, Stavros came to where my sister and I were seated.

"We will go for dinner at our cousin's Peris' restaurant. Leonarthe, my sister will tell you how to get there. I am leaving right now to go and help set the place up. I will see you guys later. Don't be overly late."

"Are all these people coming?" Angela asked.

"No. Only our close family will come," Stavros answered before leaving us to go and talk to Troy. After talking to her for a few minutes he left the restaurant.

The people started to leave. On their way out they passed by our table and offered their sympathies to us. Suddenly, Auntie shouted.

"DO YOU SEE THAT BEAUTIFUL MAN OVER THERE? DO YOU?" she was pointing at me. Two women stood in front of her looking confused and shy. "If you had agreed for your daughter to marry him when my Yiorgos asked you, Leonarthos would have stayed in Kalamata and my Yiorgos would have been happy. Take a look what your daughter missed. Take a look at this Adonis."

The older of the two women nodded. She looked upset and nervous as she said good-bye to Mom before following the younger one to head out of the restaurant. Auntie went silent. Mom turned toward me.

"This was Mihalina and her daughter Fani," she whispered. "When you were nineteen your uncle was trying to arrange your marriage to Fani. Her mother said that she did not want to see her only daughter move to Canada. But your uncle was hoping that the marriage would have brought you back to Kalamata."

"How exciting," I said, looking at my sister who could not help it but laugh.

It did not take long for the restaurant to be emptied of people. Ourania left with Panagiotis and I took my usual passengers in my rental car: Auntie in a haze, Mom engulfed in her sadness, Angela monitoring them both, and Troy. It was about 5:30 p.m. when we left the restaurant and it was getting darker. I asked Troy to give me directions to Peris' restaurant. She looked puzzled.

"I don't know how to get there from here," she said. "Didn't Stavros tell you how to get there?"

"No, he said you will take me there."

Troy turned to look at Auntie.

"Eleni mou," she pleaded. "Do you know how to get to Peris' restaurant from here?"

Auntie raised her head. "Where are we now?" she asked. Her words came out slowly and softly.

"We are on a street called Kalipatiras," I answered.

"Keep on going straight," Auntie suggested before resting her head back against the seat. So, I followed the street for the next twenty minutes or so until it disappeared.

"Troy, where are we?" my alarmed voice took her by surprise.

"Where is the main street?" Angela wondered from the back. "This street is very small and there are cement walls on both sides.

"Oh, Panagia mou," Troy said, bringing both of her hands to her cheeks. "Where did you bring us, Leonarthe?"

"I have no idea where we are. I only know that the main street disappeared all of a sudden, and we are in this small street that the car barely fits. Thank God, we are not in Canada or else I would expect a big Sasquatch to come out."

"We are in *Perivolakia*," Auntie announced from the back. "These are oranges that are hanging from the trees. Is it raining?"

"I can see that these are oranges, Auntie, but how am I going to drive out of this labyrinth?" No answer from the back. Auntie went silent again.

"These are nice oranges," Angela said. "They look ready to get picked."

"We should cut a couple," Troy recommended.

"I didn't come to freaking Greece for my uncle's funeral

to steal oranges from a freaking *perivoli*, you guys," I said with dismay. The silence that followed was interrupted only by the car's engine.

"My Yiorgo, who is looking from above would have cut a couple of oranges," Auntie's quivering voice broke the uncomfortable silence.

"Just get some oranges," Mom agreed calmly. "In the name of our Yiorgo."

I stopped the car. I looked Troy at first, and then the other three women in the back of the car. I put my hands up, giving up.

"Okay. Who is going to cut the oranges?"

"I will," Troy said. "Do we have a plastic bag?" No, we did not have a plastic bag as we were not good orange thieves. But to Troy's credit, she stepped out of the car, took her high heels off, and started jumping on the wet pavement trying to reach the orange tree branches, heavy with oranges, hanging from the top of the cement walls. Amidst my sister's laughter, Troy came back to ask for my help.

I turned the car's engine off but left the front lights on to brighten the darkness of the small street. Once out of the car, it did not take me long to evaluate the situation. The branches were quite high and there were two ways that we could reach the oranges. Bring the car close to the wall and climb up onto the hood or lift Troy up high. And I wasn't going to climb on a rental car's hood.

I told Troy that I was going to lift her up on top of my shoulders. She thought it was a great idea and giggled when I asked her to face the wall, open her legs wide, and lift her skirt above her knees. I bent low, placing my head between her legs and slowly raised my body until my shoulders were locked between her buttocks. Her upper legs touching my neck felt quite warm. She locked her feet behind my back as

I lifted her up, touching the wall with my hands for support and balance. She was pretty light. When I had risen to my full height, I placed my hands over her knees to control her weight better. She started laughing, saying that she was ticklish. I was not in the mood for laughs. Sternly, I asked her to hurry up.

However, although she held the front of her rolled skirt with one hand while reaching for the oranges with the other, part of her skirt still blocked my view. I asked her to direct me for I could not see where I was going.

"OH YES! Go left, my darling," she teased. "Oh, hold it right there. OH YES! That's good. What a large fruit I am cutting. It is HUUUGE! Now, move to the left, honey. Lift me up a little bit higher. OH YES! Let me sit properly on your shoulders. OH YES! This orange is so BIGGG!"

I understood her sex talk and her playfulness loud and clear.

"Stop having an orgasm and hurry up please," I demanded.

In less than five minutes, a number of oranges were cut and gathered up in her skirt. I could hear the other women laughing from inside the car. Thanks to the car's headlights, they had a clear view of Troy and I stealing the oranges.

By going down on one knee, I delivered Troy safely to the ground. She took a few seconds to come off of me, complaining that she liked being on my shoulders and she never had such a strong man so high between her legs. Finally, she emptied all the oranges into the trunk, put her shoes on, and took her seat in the front. Much to the delight of all four of them, I drove away.

Stavros came to meet us while I was parking on the street a few meters away from the taverna. He was not pleased that we were late. I did not bother to explain to him what had happened. I just apologized and said that we got lost. Inside the taverna were about twenty people, all Auntie's relatives. They were already eating served salads. We sat on an empty table set up for us. In no time, our table was full with food: salads and *poikilies* (variety of foods), and, of course, wine. We all started eating, except Auntie. She complained that she was not feeling well and that if she were to eat she would throw up. Angela suggested that Auntie might be feeling this way because of the medication she gave her. So, she asked the server to bring Auntie a glass of milk. And he did.

One hour later, we were the last remaining in the restaurant: Stavros and Soula, *Papou* Panagiotis, Auntie, Mom and Angela, Troy and I. Peris came to sit with us.

"How are you doing cousin?" he asked Auntie.

"I really want to eat my Yiorgos' oranges," Auntie said calmly in a whispery tone, lifting her head up. Peris looked at us confused.

"What oranges?" he asked.

"I will be back," Troy said, getting up.

Soon enough, she came back with a few of the stolen oranges. She started peeling them one by one and passing the fruit around for all to eat, explaining at the same time how we got them. Amongst many laughs and tears, everyone admitted that those were the best-tasting oranges ever. Uncle's Oranges at our Last Supper!

Katerina Thimouleas—My Yiayia

My Yiayia was born in Trachila, a small sea village in the Mani Peninsula (Greek: Μάνη, *Mánē)*, that is one of the three Peloponnese 'legs' extending southwards Greece's mainland. To the east of the Peninsula is the Laconian Gulf, and to the west, the Messenian Gulf. The peninsula forms a continuation of the Taygetos Mountain range, the western spine of the Peloponnese.

Within a family that saw many women being born and very few boys, Yiayia was emotionally attached to her son Yiorgo, my brother and I, the only two grandsons who lived with her amongst many female cousins. When my mom accompanied my father on one of his sailing trips, Yiayia took care of us, the boys. Yannis, my brother was six years old and I was four. There are two incidents that I remember from that time.

The first one is when my brother decided to make a swimming pool in Yiayia's small living room. He urged me to help him. I did, because the whole idea sounded like fun. So at first, we passed the water hose through the open window. Then, we stacked a few towels under the door separating the living room from the kitchen. After that, we moved the table and a few chairs across the door by the wall. Finally, we opened the gauge in the water hose, allowing the water to escape on the marble floor. As the water was accumulating we took our clothes off and started to slide freely on the floor on our backs or stomachs. That was more fun than I could have ever imagined.

Yiayia, who always kept track of time when she would not see us around, started to search for us. She asked Auntie Kaliopi if she saw us. The answer was negative. She asked our cousin, Aggeliki if she saw us. The answer was negative. Yiayia started to worry. "Where could the boys be?" she asked herself. She started looking around the cottages. Then she noticed the water hose leading to the window. And she heard the laughs and screams coming from her living room. She climbed the six wooden stairs leading to the kitchen and she grabbed the doorknob of the living room's door. She hesitated for a moment. Then she opened the door.

Yiayia put her hands up high, letting out a terrified scream as the water rushed through her slippers, through the kitchen floor, through the open kitchen door, and down the stairs. Her hands covered her cheeks, her eyes wide open. She shouted in dismay "Boys, what have you done?"

In the aftermath that followed, Yannis explained to her that we just wanted to clean the gleaming marble floor and make it spotless for her. That is why we poured water inside the room up to our ankles. We were forgiven and got treats as well for our trouble. However, we had to promise that next time we would let Yiayia know ahead of time when we wanted to help her with the cleaning of the house.

In the second incident, Yannis decided that he wanted to get into Yiayia's kitchen cupboard to eat her homemade watermelon *kombosta* (compote). The only problem was that the cupboard was quite high and locked with a key. The key was in Yiayia's pocket, along with many other keys. There were two ways that we could get access to the *kombosta* jars, according to Yannis. To get the key from Yiayia's pocket—it was best to do that when she was asleep, open the cupboard, get one or two jars out, eat the fruit in the syrup, lock the cupboard again, and replace the key in Yiayia's pocket. Or, we could get a small hammer, break the glass in the cupboard, take one or two jars out, eat the fruit in the syrup, and blame someone else.

That's when our cousin Aggeliki came into the picture. At twelve years old, she was not the smartest cookie in the neighborhood. But she was taller than Yannis and I. On top of a chair she could easily reach the cupboard. She was willing to help us with the agreement that she could have one jar of watermelon *kombosta* all by herself.

We could not find a hammer but we did get a brick instead. We waited when Yiayia and auntie Kaliopi were busy in the taverna. We closed the kitchen door and we pushed a chair up close to the cupboard. Aggeliki climbed on the chair, reached the cupboard, and broke the glass with the brick, cutting her hand in the process. She dropped the brick on the floor and started to cry in pain. As she tried to come down off the chair, Yannis demanded that she get him a jar. With tears in her eyes and some blood dripping on her clothes, she got a jar out of the cupboard and handed it to him. Then she jumped down from the chair and ran out of the kitchen screaming and holding her hand. Yannis opened the jar and started eating the fruit as fast as he could, using his hands. I was terrified but not terrified enough to refuse when he offered me a couple of pieces of fruit. And then Yiayia, Auntie and Aggeliki, still crying with a handkerchief around her hand, showed up just as Yannis hid the jar under the kitchen sink.

I started to cry. Yannis held me, comforting me. What a bad cousin, Aggeliki was to make his little brother watch her break the glass in the cupboard to steal the *komposta,* he recounted to Auntie Kaliopi.

"I tried to tell her not to do it, but she wouldn't listen," he said to Yiayia.

Auntie Kaliopi bent Aggeliki forward and with a heavy hand, smacked her behind a couple of times. She lifted my cousin up, holding her from her midsection and carried her outside. We could hear Aggeliki screaming her innocence. Yiayia held me. She kissed me softly and calmed me down. She opened the cupboard and reached for a jar. My brother and I sat on the table and had some extra *komposta* while watching Yiayia clean up the broken glass.

In her last years of her life, Yiayia suffered from Parkinson's and irritable hot flashes that would make her take off all of her clothes and walk onto the balcony for some fresh air, much to the delight and laughs of the neighborhood kids. I would hide behind the curtains and beg her to come inside the house.

"Pissto thialo Loumbarthe," she would angrily mispronounce my name and wiggle her cane at me. That was her way of saying 'get lost' or 'go away', although her words might also be interpreted as 'go to hell'. Nevertheless, she would not leave the balcony unless I would go out and grab her hand to lead her back into the house, amidst the neighborhood children's ridicule.

Mom had me sleep in the same room with Yiayia, with two single beds separated by a half of a meter distance.

Almost every night the following would occur. Yiayia would wake me up, poking me with her cane. She would either ask me to fix her pillows or help her get up to use the washroom. Fixing the pillows was not such a problem. I would climb on her bed, push her body up, and in the few seconds I had, rearrange and fluff up her three pillows. Then, I would go back to sleep.

However, getting her to the washroom was daunting. It required a manipulation of her body weight to help her stand. Then, using one hand to hold her cane and the other to partly lean on me, she would lead me to the washroom. She would take her time peeing; sometimes she would not pee at all. In any case, I would get the opportunity to get into the bathtub and fall asleep until her cane poking would wake me up to take her back to the room.

Eventually, sleep deprivation caught up with me and I became sick. Mom realized what was going on and she substituted for me. Yet, during the day and when I was available, I would always be around Yiayia, helping out with bringing her water or feeding her or assisting with any other needs she may have had.

I did not witness her passing but I do remember Uncle George, Mom, and Auntie Kaliopi being in the room when that happened. I saw Uncle coming out from the room with tears in his eyes. He wiped them right away when he saw me as if ashamed to show his sadness. That was the first time I had ever seen Uncle crying.

Yiayia's funeral was a simple one. I was not allowed to witness her casket carrying or to go to the church. But Yiayia did visit me in my dreams for quite a few years after her death, mostly waving at me or telling me stories and poems as she used to do when she was alive; stories about the big metal men that would walk amongst us one day, and

Homer's *Iliad* poems about the Trojan Wars. On occasion, she would also appear in Mom's dreams as well, offering words of guidance or words of caution.

Troy's Manifestion

Wednesday morning, Mom, Angela, and I, were having our morning coffee in the covered area of the penthouse's balcony. Now that the funeral was out of the way, Mom seemed to be more relaxed and ready to engage in conversation.

"You know," Mom said, taking a sip of the hot liquid, "your aunt told me that she wanted to have her name alongside your uncle's name on the tombstone."

"Really?" Angela said, raising her eyebrows. "That's highly irregular and it makes no sense. What would they write on the stone? That she is still alive?"

"It makes no sense," I agreed. "The tombstones are for the dead people."

"I know," Mom nodded. "I told her that this cannot be done. So she decided to have a poem she wrote, chiseled on the stone. I told her that she needs to stay strong for her father who will very soon be in much need of her help. It is like a dream that my brother is not with us any longer. It is like a dream."

We all kept quiet for a few minutes. I noticed that there were no noisy birds chirping away across the park. The dark clouds in the sky were threatening to burst at any time. For some reason I started thinking about my children.

"Have you talked to your husband and the kids?" I asked my sister.

"I will call them later on, for sure," she replied. "What about you?"

"I will call my home later on as well. I am missing my guys."

"It's too bad that your uncle and aunt could not have any children," Mom interrupted. "They left no seeds behind." She was looking visibly sad.

"Well, for sure they will not leave any 'seeds' behind of their own but their DNA exists within other people," I remarked. "I mean, Uncle's DNA or at least part of it is within me, because of you; and Auntie's DNA or at least part of it can be found within her cousins."

"Your uncle is dead and without children his death is final," Mom cautioned me. "The only thing that will leave with us is his spirit, his memory."

"That is one way to see it, Mom," Angela said. "And that is the view of how people see it. But Leo is correct, speaking from a scientific point of view."

"For sure," I agreed. "I actually think that our brother's DNA, is more of a George Thimouleas' DNA than a Hutchinson's DNA. How many people thought that our brother was Uncle's son?"

"Your uncle loved your brother Yanni. And he loved all of you like his own children," Mom whispered. "Many times he did not know how to show his love toward you guys. But he loved you very much."

"Like the times he would chase Yanni and I around the soccer fields of the town?" I laughed at my own sentence, causing Mom and Sister to laugh as well.

"He did not want you to become bums and give up your education for soccer," Mom said. "He thought that all soccer players had no brains and were useless."

I laughed again because the memory of my uncle chasing me around the 'coal' soccer field in 1976 was something that I treasured. I started telling the story to Mom and Angela.

In the summer of 1976, I visited Kalamata for the first time after we had moved to Oinoussai Island in 1974. There was an open area across the Mylos, where the City Park is located now, and there were only a few bushes and trees along Psaron Street. The trains still came all the way to the port to pick up wheat and coal. But because sometimes the coal was too much and trains were not available, small trucks carried it from the port to the open area, creating small coal mountains. As trains became available and workers loaded them up with coal, a black powder field was left behind and hence, created a soccer field for the neighborhood children. Around the coalfield, thorny bushes were crawling along the ground, ready to punish anyone who was not careful going through them. The thorns would tag along on pants or shoes and created instant pain when penetrated flesh.

I had never played soccer on a coalfield before. When my friends invited me to play, although I had suffered a knee injury riding my bike, I did not refuse the invitation. Uncle had done a great job to bandage my knee anyways.

A bathing suit and a pair of runners is all that we needed to play under the hot sun. Two sets of two wooden poles on either end of the field served as goalposts as the game started. It was fun for me initially, trying to maneuver the soccer ball through the black thin dust that crept up in the hot air. However, soon enough my breathing became heavy as my nostrils got extremely dry. I started complaining to my teammates. But they had everything under control. They directed me toward a big plastic barrel, full of water that was positioned on one of the sides of the field. It was not for drinking; it was there so players could dunk their head for a few seconds under the water, to get some relief from the heat and the coal dust.

I leaned over the barrel and checked the water. It was not clean by any means, rather black-ish. Who knew when was the last time that it had been changed. Probably my friends kept adding water to the barrel rather than cleaning it and replenishing it after every game. But that would do, I thought.

I dunked my head under the water for a few seconds. The water was hot from the sun. As I pulled my head out of the barrel, pushing my wet hair with both of my hands toward the back of my head, the water drops ran freely down my shoulders and the rest of my body. I watched black water streamlines form on my chest creeping all the way down to my bathing suit. All the players were dirty due to the coal dust sticking onto their sweaty bodies. I took my knee bandages off before I entered the game again. They were black anyway and they were restricting my soccer moves.

And then I heard Uncle. He was on the sidelines by the railway tracks commanding me to stop playing. He was freaked out that my knee was not bandaged and, about my audacity playing soccer. The game he hated.

I refused to listen to him and told him to go home. Much to my dismay, he took off his sandals and threw them in my direction one at a time. My friends stopped playing and started to laugh. In the far distance, from the balcony of his apartment building, I could hear Auntie calling him to leave me alone.

Uncle was insisting that I leave the field. He could not believe it that he had taken time to care for my knee and I just jumped into the coal dirt to damage it further. To my response, that it was my knee and I would do whatever I wanted to it, he just lost it. He picked up a rock from the ground and threw it at me. I jumped over the bouncing rock, grimacing and laughing at the same time. I dared him to come and get *me. He took the challenge seriously only to discover that there were many thorns on the ground spiking his feet. He started to swear, tippy-toeing around the many thorns. And between the swearing, he would scream at Auntie to get back in the house and mind her own business.*

Finally, the pain produced from the thorns and the blood dripping through his toes made him back off to safer ground. I felt sorry and apologetically threw his sandals back to him. He raised his fist and warned me that we would talk again at home. I agreed. And then I continued playing the wonderful game.

Later on, at home, Auntie stood between us. She announced in a defiant way that he needed to understand that I was sixteen, a bright student, and an excellent athlete. Uncle had no business interfering with whatever sports I was playing, Auntie declared. And, since that time, Uncle never bothered me again about playing or following soccer. And soccer, for me, became a way of life.

I finished my story and realized that Mom and Sister had tears in their eyes from laughing so much. I wasn't trying to be funny. I was just describing the incident. Uncle's logic was mysteriously on the wrong path, we decided. He wished for me to be a very good student but without being involved in soccer, my favorite sport. It was incomprehensible to him that I could be a very good student and a very good athlete at the same time.

"I guess what ancient Greeks believed Uncle did not," Mom said. "That a healthy mind is in a healthy body. And that is why we need to exercise our bodies: to keep our mind healthy. "

"Well, that is not a completely correct statement," I countered. "As far as I am concerned, we do talk about two different things here: the body and our thinking ability, if you will, that may not necessarily coexist in a healthy collaborative environment. One of the most famous examples is Stephen Hawking. A genius mind trapped in a sick body.

Another example is my daughter Marialina. She has a body, that by many accounts appears healthy, but her thinking ability is dramatically developmentally behind due to her suffering from epilepsy."

"That's well said," Angela agreed. "As a physician, at times, I have to differentiate between mind and body to understand my patients' suffering better. Of course, body suffering could influence the thinking ability and vice versa."

"Sure. And that's where the death paradox is coming to place," I said. "When someone dies, for sure, the body is gone. Is the thinking ability gone as well? The brain is gone. It's dead. But is the thinking ability gone?"

"Of course it is," Mom agreed, leaning back in her chair. "The thinking ability exists because the brain exists. With the brain dead the thinking ability is gone. There is no 'mind'."

I scratched my head. I leaned forward over the coffee table and stared into Mom's eyes. I spoke slowly.

"So, if we could extract Uncle's brain from his head and keep it 'alive' with some sort of a mechanism, would that suffice to argue that his thinking ability is also alive?"

"I don't know," Mom replied. "I am going to cook for lunch." She got up and walked inside the living room. Sister got up and followed behind her.

"Too philosophical for me," she said. "I am going to help Mom."

"Would you say Uncle George would be a good ghost?" I posed the question.

"I don't know. Why don't you ask him? You have part of his DNA," Angela said jokingly before going through the balcony doors.

I posed the same question to Troy later on in the afternoon when we were having cappuccinos at Café Botega, in

Platia Agiou Georgiou, which is in the city's center. But Troy was not interested to talk about ghosts and death. She would rather talk about us, as she pointed out. With a sad face she held my hand. I felt her foot under the table touching my leg.

"What's going to happen to us?" she asked with a baby-like voice. "What are you planning to do?"

"I do not understand the question, Troy," I muttered. "I haven't given up fixing what is broken with my marriage. I will certainly try to work things out when I get back to Vancouver."

"But you know that I love you," she said. "You know I do, since we were kids."

"That was long time ago, you silly. I can't commit to any relationship when I am in a relationship that is called marriage. And I don't think you love me either. It is just an infatuation."

"But when we kissed it meant nothing?"

"Troy, when we kissed it was purely accidental. Don't you think?"

"No, it was not. Our bodies wanted each other like the desert wants the rain."

"Well, I don't know if I am the desert or the rain but my brain does not agree with my body. So, I suppose...."

"So, we cannot be together?" she interrupted me, raising her voice. "Like you came back to my life after so many years and you don't want to be together?"

"Are you okay? Keep your voice down. This is crazy. Are you kidding me, Troy?" I said, allowing a nervous laugh to escape through my lips.

"Are you hot for that woman in the car Leonarthe? Is that it? Or are you interested for my little cousin who works at Kastraki? I hope not! You don't want to go back to your crazy wife. DO YOU? You know that she will not take care of you like I will."

She was talking too fast. Her voice was in distress.

I put both hands on the table and by leaning forward, I focused on her eyes trying to see if she was serious or not. This conversation is going nowhere I thought. Her face had a serious look; her hands gripped the coffee mug.

"Troy," I said, with a delicate emphasis to my words, "you are absolutely making no sense. In fact, you are re-minding me of my wife as she will go on talking without a breath and with no interest to communicate. What's gotten into you? If I misled you, I am sorry. But honey, I am not interested to get involved in any relationship. We were friends since we were kids. Don't you remember? Even George the blind man used to say, 'Hey Loni, where is your friend Eleni?' I mean, I can't see you as anything else but as a friend. I hope you are okay with that."

"I don't understand," she cried. "Every time I hold your hand, I feel your blood running through my veins. Every time you talk, I want to seal your lips with mine. When you lifted me up on your shoulders yesterday, I was on top of the world. It can be no other woman for you but me. I love you. The kiss! Our kiss was not a lie. If it was, tell me it was, and I will believe you. But trust me when I tell you that I cannot live without you. I need your love. Without it, I will not survive. My life would be meaningless. I don't want this to happen!"

I was flabbergasted. I put my hands up in despair. Were those tears in her eyes?

"ELENI," I raised my voice with authority. "You don't want what to happen? Nothing has happened. Nothing will happen. I am offering you my friendship. I love you as a friend. The kiss was a mistake. What do you want from me?"

I stopped talking because I felt I was getting angrier by the moment. She flipped her dirty blonde hair to the side of her face. Her big eyes completed her poker face. Was she getting angry now? I got ready to hear the worst. And then she started laughing. And laughing not with a nervous laugh or a laugh produced from despair but with a hysterical, rather happy laugh. What a nutty, I thought.

"Was something I said funny?" I asked her.

"You are funny," she said. "I was just pulling your leg. I was joking. Agape mou, you fell for it so badly. You should have seen your face. Oh, Panagia mou! You believed every word I said."

I leaned back and let my body relax on the chair. Yes, she was right. She got me there for a moment. But I did not find the past half an hour or so funny, as my head was hurting and my mouth felt extremely dry. I drank the glass of water in front of me.

"Phew, Troy," I said rubbing my forehead. "No sex for you then."

"Hey. That's too big of a punishment," she complained going back to her baby voice. "I haven't had sex for years. Can't you give me some?"

"Stop it," I said, getting the last sip of my coffee before standing up. "Let's go home. I had enough of you." I walked toward the door.

"Hey," she muttered, pushing the chair backward with her bum and standing up. "Are you angry at me? Come on! I was kidding. Loni, I was just kidding. Please wait."

She ran after me and when she reached me, she put her hands around my mid-section, holding me tight from behind. She rested her head between my shoulder blades and she brought my movement to a stop.

"I am sorry," she whispered. "That was mean of me. I

am sorry."

I loosened her hand's grip and turned around. I moved her face slightly up by raising her chin, using my right index and thumb fingers. I kissed her gently: the right eye first, then the left, and finally her lips.

"That is to remind you that what you just did was stupid," I said, hugging her warmly. "I think I cannot be angry at you. Not for too long anyway."

"That's nice. I know you love me, deep, deep, inside. We were born to be together but life is cruel and separated us from the get-go. Wouldn't you say I am correct, Loni?"

I held her hand not responding to her question. I led the walk through the Platia, enjoying the many lights intercepting us from all sort of angles, and amongst many other people who were romancing the wetness of the night.

"You mentioned George the blind man. Do you remember George?" Troy asked, breaking the silence. "Do you remember how we were trying to fool him? I would try to mimic your voice and you were trying to sound like me."

"Yes. I remember. My other uncle, George Kalouthis, my aunt Kaliopi's husband who died years ago, tried many times to fool him as well by pretending he was a woman. He would say with a high-pitched voice, 'George I love you.' But George the blind man would laugh and say, 'Kalouthi, you don't smell like a woman.'"

"How did he die again?"

"My uncle? He died from liver cancer. I was fortunate to come to Kalamata from the island that summer before his death and spend some quality time with him. He was bedbound at his home and appreciated my company very much as I was his 'favorite little boy'. "

"You are such a good boy," Troy said holding my hand.

"Yes. Now, Troy, please keep quite. Let us walk quietly."

I felt her hand gripping mine every bit stronger. She kept quiet all the way home. Then she broke the silence again.

"Kalinixta agape mou," she whispered in my ear, giving me a hug and a kiss on the cheek. "And I meant everything I said." She left me standing on the pavement.

The Two Georges

George—The Blind Man

I remember George the blind man walking up and down Psaron Street, with a Charlie Chaplin slow walk (but holding no cane). The palm of his right hand moved side to side, in an autistic way, in front of his nose, pinching and slapping his cheek from time to time. His head slightly pointed upward. George was born blind but he did not consider himself disabled for he could do some things better than others who could see. Yet, he was always thankful when people would help him out on occasion. For instance, although he knew how to count his money by feeling the coins, he was appreciative when, after a purchase, the correct change was handed back to him.

Everyone in the neighborhood and most people in Kalamata knew George. And he could remember names by listening to one's voice only once. There were so many times that myself and my childhood friend Eleni tried to fool him by faking our voices and pretending we were others, but every time he would identify us. This unique memorization served him well as he would draw small crowds reciting poems and short stories when he was in the mood.

George liked me and he considered me his 'kid' friend. He also liked my Aunt Kaliopi. They were born on the same day, but, "She is fatter than I am," he would often declare. Yet, I am sure he never had the chance to touch her to reaffirm his statement.

She operated my Yiayia's taverna, my aunt. As a six year old, one of my chores was to guide George to the taverna so he could have a glass of retsina. Or two! Or three! He would get drunk sometimes. But at all times he was happy and he enjoyed singing along to the jukebox songs playing, clicking his tongue to the bouzouki rhythm. That is what my aunt wanted him to do anyway to create a sense of happiness in the taverna's atmosphere. "No singing, no retsina," she would tease him, laughing!

In a way, the taverna was the Port's and *Milos's* workers' social club, most of them men. There were a few women hanging around at times, called *koritsia* (young girls), who for money or a free drink, would offer kisses and perhaps something more to the men. However, they would not call themselves prostitutes. In fact, they would get very offended if anyone would dare calling them that 'dirty word' as they did not feel obligated to accept money or offer themselves to anyone if they did not want to. They would refer to themselves as 'healers of loneliness' or 'free women' or 'women for love', 'working' Monday to Saturday but never on Sunday. Sunday was a resting day.

There was this undisputed respect that single or married

men had for the *koritsia*. The unwritten code was that whatever happens in the taverna stays in the taverna. However, that did not minimize fights between some men and their wives whom, through the neighborhood gossip, found out that their husband possibly had sex with one of the *koritsia*.

Within this social environment George was accepted and humored by the men who sometimes would make fun of his blindness or his drunkenness. I would watch him pinching his red cheek and with his closed eyes focusing blindly on the taverna's ceiling, laughing at questions such as: "Yiorgo, do you pee your pants when you are drunk?" Or, "Yiorgo, do you have a girlfriend?" Or, "Yiorgo, did you fight the Germans in the war?" George, holding his own ground, would make fun of the men's inabilities, one of which was, that they could not make love to a woman more than once per night. And that would cause a ruckus because he would make the point suggesting that he could certainly do that; and the men would tease him. Yet, Maria, one of the *koritsia*, could attest that this was certainly true! She was the one who, many times, would walk George from the taverna to his home.

George never had to pay for his drinking. There was always someone who would pay for him and if there was no one around, my aunt would still fill up his glass. His drinking, however, did not make his mother, Mrs. Anna, happy. She was his primary caregiver and she had many things to worry about. She raised George without a husband—his father died soon after WWII. Also, she was not appreciative when George would get drunk and pee his pants. But she was careful enough not to express her 'disappointment' with him directly, at least, when I happened to be around. At times, Mrs. Anna gave me one drachma to secretly give an envelope to Maria. Maria would take the envelope with a smile, mess my hair with her hands, kiss me on the cheek, and say, "*Ευχαριστω ομορφουλι μου.*" (Thank you, my little cutie.) Then, she would lead George from the taverna to his home even when Nikos was around.

Nikos was a bus driver who drove the bus from the neighborhood to the city's center. He was single and Maria's friend. He would stop the bus at the exact same location, by the huge old maple tree, as there was no sign of a bus station anywhere on the street. George would wait for the bus at the same location as well. Not three meters down the street or three meters up the street. He would wait just by the tree. The discussion between Niko and George was pretty much the same every time the bus front doors would open.

"George, do you have the bus fare?"

"Hello Niko. How are you? Can I pay you tomorrow?"

"Okay. Come in. Now, watch your step." (I do not think George ever paid the bus fare!)

George would orient himself by touching the outside of the bus, finding the door's opening, grabbing the rail, and slowly climbing the two stairs to get inside the bus. When inside he would sit on the very first seat and, if the first seat was occupied, Niko would ask the passenger to move for George's sake.

George would do much of the shopping for his mother as he traveled in the city either by foot or by bus. At every instance, he knew where he was and recognized places like the farmer's market, the butcher's shop, the baker's shop, and the church (his task was to light a candle and ask God for forgiveness) by the noise level. When shopping or walking about he was careful not to overspend his money or to fall prey to the gypsy kids who always tried to pick his pockets.

He did not like the gypsy kids. He called them '*αλητες*'

(bad kids) and he could 'smell' them. His ability was remarkable in that even if he was in a crowded place he could 'smell' and 'feel' and 'touch' his way through the crowd; or perhaps the crowd would move around him. In a snapshot, it looked like people were not paying attention to him or rather his ability to navigate through the crowd was not anything to pay attention to. Was it because of his disability that he had this ability? Also, if George had no prior knowledge of how the ability to see enables others, for simply that 'ability' was never a part of him, would he then perceive or consider himself as having a disability? These were questions that I often wondered about.

Cars provided a different challenge for George altogether. He could not run or move fast by nature. Not that he knew what running was anyway. So, if he would hear a car he would freeze (in the middle of the road if that was the path he was on) and look fiercely disoriented. Drivers who knew him patiently waited until he moved. Sometimes they came out of the car, moved him to the side, and then proceeded with their business. Drivers who did not know him were challenged to drive around him, on occasion, sound the car horn.

"Don't you see I am blind? Στραβομαλάκες (blind jerks)?" He would scream and swear at them. There were many such times that I, and the other kids, would run and guide him to safety.

I do not remember who told me or how I found out that George died. Apparently, a truck driver parked on the side of the road did not realize that George was walking behind the truck. When the driver started the engine, George froze as he would always do. The truck backed up, killing him instantly. A few of us kids were outside his house watching the adults pay their respects while Mrs. Anna and Maria were crying. When Maria saw me she called me close to her. She started messing up my hair with her rough hands. She said, "We're going to miss my little brother *ομορφουλι μου* (My little cutie). Aren't we?" She left the town a few days after. Mrs. Anna passed away a couple of months later. Maria, to my surprise, did not attend her mother's funeral, organized by the state.

Uncle George Kalaouthis—The Interview

ME: Thank you for agreeing to be interviewed, Uncle.

UNCLE: That's okay. I feel important. Like a movie star, you know. Like Marlon Brando. *He laughs.*

ME: The way we are going to do this is as follows. I will ask you certain questions and I will also state some facts. If you disagree or have anything different to say, please say it. I will tape everything so that I can print it after. Is that okay?

UNCLE: Go ahead. I have never done anything like this before. It would be my first and my last interview.

He coughs. He uses a blue handkerchief to clean the blood coming out of his mouth.

ME: You were born in the island of Samos. Can you tell me a little bit about your childhood?

UNCLE: I was born in Karlovasi. The city is about 32 kilometers Northwest on the island of Samos. I think the Turks gave the city that name; it means snow fallen plain. My dad called the city Karlovas. I remember the beautiful beaches, small and large, with a mixture of sand and pebbles. You know, as a child I used to go with my friends to Potami Beach, a few kilometers from the town. We used to play in the waterfalls and the lagoons for hours.

My dad was of the clan Kalouthis. He named me George after his father. I had three sisters. I finished the elementary school and I started working in a fishing boat. I was twelve years old, you know… tough years then. WWII had made the life miserable for everyone.

ME: How did you meet auntie Kaliopi?

UNCLE: With the fishing boat we came to Kalamata to sell the fish. I was done with fishing. I saw the *Mylos* by the Port and I went to ask for a job. They wanted strong hands to carry the wheat and they hired me on the spot. I was seventeen years old at the time. Strong and tall, I was.

One day I went with the other workers for a drink in your Yiayia's taverna. Kaliopi was working there. Making the food and pouring the wine. She looked straight into my eyes and said, 'What do you want?' I said. 'You, I want'.

I kept going to the taverna. Your Yiayia did not like it a bit. But your aunt was interested.

ME: WWII was over by then right?

UNCLE: Yes, it was. But the *Emfýlios Pólemos*, (The Civil War) was starting between the government's army—backed by the English and the Americans, and the Communist Party, KKE, backed by Yugoslavia's Tito, and Albania.

ME: Were you involved in that?

UNCLE: No, I was not. I was too much in love and I didn't care about all that crap. But many Mylos' workers were involved, and divided.

ME: You got married when you were twenty. Right? And Auntie was seventeen.

UNCLE: Yes. Give or take a year or so.

ME: I believe you got a cottage as a dowry?

UNCLE: Yes. But that was nothing. Kaliopi was working the taverna and I was working in the *Mylos*. We extended the cottage later on anyways to house your three cousins.

ME: You had three daughters: Vassiliki, Katerina, and Aggeliki. Also Auntie had a miscarriage.

UNCLE: She lost my son.

ME: What do you mean, 'She lost your son'?

UNCLE: Her first pregnancy was a boy. But she was doing the wine and moving the heavy barrels, and she lost my son. After that I was jinxed. Three girls!

ME: Did you have a problem having girls?

UNCLE: I always wanted a boy. Look at your family. Your father, although he was an Englishman, he had two boys right away. How can this be?

ME: Well, I don't think being an Englishman had to do anything with this. But I know that especially in our parts of Greece, here in Mani, boys are considered a blessing, especially by their own mothers and grandmothers. Is it because you had three girls you started drinking?

UNCLE: No. It had nothing to do with that. Most workers from Mylos were drinking heavily to forget their life's pains. I was a heavy smoker and drinker even before I met your aunt.

ME: I seem to remember some big fights you had with Auntie Kaliopi. Can you talk about them?

UNCLE: Most of our fights were about my way of life and her way of controlling. But since we are talking about births, I will tell you that one of our fights was when you were born.

ME: Really? Tell me more.

UNCLE: Your mother, by the way, I have great respect for her, did not have an easy pregnancy with you. Katerina (*my Yiayia*), figured out that your mother was going to labor. Maria (*my mother*) ignored her; but Katerina came and woke Kaliopi and me. She asked Kaliopi to take your mother to the hospital, and that she did.

I don't know if your mother told you but you were coming with the legs down and the doctor had to turn you around so your head would come first. And that was very painful for your mother. In fact, after you came out there was some time gone by that you did not cry. Maria thought you were dead. Also, she was bleeding heavily and the doctor said to 'Forget about the newborn. Save the mother'. But eventually the bleeding stop, you started to cry, and all was well. Anyways, listen, my mouth is dry. Would you mind getting me a glass of water?

ME: Would you like to take a break? I see you are getting tired.

He raised his body a little bit higher on the bed. Slowly but steadily he fixed the two pillows behind his back to properly support himself.

UNCLE: I am getting tired, but that's okay. A glass of water would be great.

After ten minutes.

ME: Can we continue now?

UNCLE: Yes. Thank you for the water. The freaking blood taste in my mouth drives me nuts.

ME: You were talking about my birth causing a fight between you and Auntie.

UNCLE: She came back from the hospital all happy announcing that 'Maria had another boy.' I looked at her and said, 'Why can't you have a boy?' And that stirred a fight.

ME: I don't get it. By that time you already had three girls. Aggeliki, the youngest, was eight years old.

UNCLE: But I wanted to keep trying for a boy and she would not want to have any more children. She would not give me a son.

ME: I think, I may as well inform you that it is the man's sperm that is the common denominator if the woman conceives a boy or a girl.

UNCLE: So what? My sperm was fine. We just needed to try again.

ME: Let's change the subject. Can you tell me about your relationship with my dad and my uncle George Thimouleas?

UNCLE: I considered your dad my buddy. He called me 'brother' you know. And, in fact, we would drink a couple of glasses of wine together. But Thimouleas, Kaliopi's brother, was a jerk.

ME: I know you guys had a couple of fights.

UNCLE: What fights? One time he attacked me when I was drunk and I did not know what the heck was going on.

ME: I believe, you were physical with Auntie.

UNCLE: So, what? That's an issue between a husband and a wife. He had no reason to attack me. Why he did not do this when was I sober?

ME: Well, you were hitting his sister. Right?

UNCLE: False. She was hitting me. Have you seen your auntie lately? Can you imagine any man being able to hit her?

ME: Yes, but when this fight occurred was years ago. Not lately. You were violent then when you were drinking.

UNCLE: Nephew, I can tell you that there were two times that I called the police and complained about your auntie beating me up. They laughed at me.

ME: Yes, but you were drunk in both of those occasions. My understanding is that the policemen came and told you to sober up before you press charges. And you never did press charges.

UNCLE: Whatever! She made my life miserable at times.

ME: But she is taking care of you now that you are very sick. Isn't she?

UNCLE: She has no choice. I was the man of her life. Why do you think she named the taverna after my last name? Do you know that she has not being nice to my Vostok rocket for years now?

Vostok was the first spaceflight of the Vostok Soviet Union pro-gramme, and the first manned spaceflight in history. On April 12, 1961, the Vostok 3KA space capsule with Soviet cosmonaut Yuri Gagarin completed an orbit around Earth.

ME: Are you referring to not having sex? I presume you have nicknamed your penis Vostok?

UNCLE: Yes.

ME: Did you ever have an affair?

UNCLE: Never.

ME: But you accused Auntie of having affairs.

UNCLE: There were many men coming in the taverna. Do you know how many times I caught her having conversations with men?

ME: She was serving her customers Uncle. Many of them were family friends. Auntie knew everyone's business because she made it her business to listen to everyone's woes and troubles. She cared for people; I know at times she kept families together by intervening in a positive way. All the times you accused her of cheating, you were drunk as a skunk. At least that's what Yiayia told me.

UNCLE: Katerina never liked me. She never wanted me to be her son-in-law.

ME: You did forbid her entering the taverna. Even though, practically, she owned it.

UNCLE: I forbid her coming because every time she would come, she would somehow be the cause of Kaliopi and me starting a fight.

ME: Do you recall when I was four years old and I was lost for a few hours? You are the one who found me.

UNCLE: Everyone was frantic because we could not find you. Especially your Yiayia was screaming like crazy. You were a boy, you see. She loved you and your brother

Yanni. If anything would have happened to you 'boys' she would have gone mad.

She was going up and down the neighborhood calling your name. And then she wanted to go to the gypsy camp and check their tents to make sure that they did not abduct you.

Anyways, something told me to check in the wine cellar. There you were, seating on your butt, opening and closing the barrel spout and tasting the wine. There was wine all over the floor and you were very drunk. But everyone was glad I found you. You were asleep for the next two days. Overdosed!

He laughs and coughs at the same time. He covers his mouth with the handkerchief.

He coughs some blood into the handkerchief.

ME: When did you find out about your liver cancer?

UNCLE: A couple of months ago. I knew something was wrong with me.

ME: But you stopped drinking and smoking a few years ago.

UNCLE: Yes, but the damage was done.

ME: The doctor said you have two to three months to live.

UNCLE: I am going to go in two to three weeks.

He laughs. He drinks water from the glass.

ME: Why do you say that?

UNCLE: Because the blood is dark now. That means my liver is gone.

ME: Are you scared of dying?

UNCLE: I am not scared at all. What good would that do? Being scared? What for? When the time will come, I will close my eyes and say goodbye to this freaking world forever. You know, my eyes have seen a lot. Mostly misery! I

HAD ENOUGH!

ME: Do you believe in God?

UNCLE: When I was a child I used to go to the church. Then, one day, the priest took me and my friend in his house. I was ten at the time. Then he told us that God is good and God is great and we are his children. And all of these crap… before going down on his knees to kiss our genitals.

ME: WOW! That's terrible. Was he gay?

UNCLE: He was gay and a child molester.

ME: Did you tell anyone?

UNCLE: I told my father. He beat the heck out of me for 'coming out with that lie'. So, NO! I don't believe there is a God.

He closes his eyes. He sighs.

ME: Well, because people are bad that does not mean there is no God. And because that priest was bad that does not mean that all priests are bad.

UNCLE: People have done many atrocities in the name of A GOD.

ME: And many good things….

He interrupts.

UNCLE: Who cares? There is no hell or heaven. We die. We are gone. Good on the folks who stay behind.

ME: Would you say you have accomplished what you wanted to accomplish in the span of your life?

UNCLE: My life was simple. Yes, I ended up an alcoholic, but in retrospect, I think I was drinking to forget life's misery.

ME: So, are you happy you are dying? I don't get it.

UNCLE: I am not happy about it. But I am not sad either. I just don't care about dying.

ME: What about leaving your loved ones behind? Do you

care about Auntie Kaliopi and your daughters?

UNCLE: Of course. But they would be okay without me. I bet they may not have very fond memories of my past behavior. They are all adults. They would be okay.

ME: To end this interview, is there anything else you want to tell me?

UNCLE: One advice I have for you. Live your life as it comes. Do not complicate it.

ME: Thank you for the interview, Uncle.

UNCLE: No, thank you!

He gives me a hug!

Episode 10

The American Women

My sister rented a cab and left for Athens two days after Uncle's funeral. I wished I could go with her but unfortunately my flight was not due for two more days and the cost to change the ticket was too much. Mom would not want to leave just yet anyway. I asked my sister when in Vancouver to visit my wife and tell her what had transpired because the couple of times I had called home, my wife kept asking, 'Do you have fun Leo?' And I did not have fun.

I decided to go to the Jumbo store by the port, at the end of Psaron Street, to shop for souvenirs. When I was done, I stopped by the Electra Hotel across the street from Jumbo. I asked the young lady in reception if it was possible to call Lita's room so that I could talk to her. But she informed me that Lita and her friends were out. Before leaving, I left a note for the Americans, as I had named them, to meet me at Kastraki at 7:30 p.m.

Eleni greeted me with a big smile when she saw me

entering the cafeteria. She looked great wearing slim black pants and a tight white top promoting her well-defined body.

"Back to Kastraki, I see," she said. "Did you miss me?"

"Not really. I am waiting for some friends to show up."

"That's not nice," she said grimacing, putting on a sad face. "And I thought that we could have fun together."

"Oh, we can have fun alright. But do not advertise it to your cousin Eleni because she would not be happy. And I don't think it's me she would blame."

She giggled. She flipped her ponytail to the side and looked sternly at me.

"All of my cousins are just jealous because I am younger and prettier," she said. "What would you like to drink, Leo?"

"I will have a hot Grand Marnier please."

I followed her movements as she slowly poured hot water into the small round glass. Then she emptied the water into the sink before pouring two to three ounces of the liqueur back into the glass. She handed me the beverage over the bar leaning slightly forward. She flipped her ponytail to the side again.

"Don't you find me attractive, Leo?"

"Extremely," I replied. "But I am not sure what you are looking for? I smell a trap and a lot of trouble. I cannot even allow my imagination to interfere with what your body language is proposing to me right now."

"What is my body language proposing?" she asked with a seductive and cleverly hidden sarcastic tone, clearly playing with me. My eyes shifted from my glass to her face and down to her body parts that kept moving, it seemed, in a very slow motion. I smiled. I took her right hand in my hands and kissed it gently. From the corner of my eyes I saw the Americans entering the cafeteria. They came straight to the bar.

"I see you are busy my dear," Lita said teasingly in English. "You couldn't even wait for us to have fun." I stood up from my stool and gave her a hug.

"Please save me," I whispered in her ear.

"Can we have three Camparis please?" Lita grudgingly ordered from Eleni. She grabbed my hand with one hand and my drink with the other. She pulled me towards a corner table by a slightly open window. Nancy and Vicki followed silently.

Eleni looked distraught, but she did start preparing the drinks.

"Who is she?" Lita asked me when we settled in our chairs.

"She is my aunt's younger cousin. She is a teaser, but I like her."

"She is too young for you, Leo. Stop it. Don't' you think so, girls?"

Vicki nodded in agreement. I decided to have some fun. When Eleni brought the drinks on a tray, I politely asked her to sit on my lap. She obeyed like a little kitten ready and waiting to be pet, much to the Americans' disbelief.

"Eleni," I said calmly. "The girls say that I am too old for you. What do you have to say to that?"

"Love has no boundaries," Eleni said confidently. "Age is in the eyes of the beholder. Age is just a number."

I squeezed her body with a cuddly bear hug.

"And there you have it," I announced to the Americans with a laugh. "She loves me and she does not care about my age." I kissed Eleni's cheek lightly and allowed her to stand up, prompting her to go back to the bar.

"Wow," Nancy said in English. "Was that rehearsed? What the heck was that about?"

"Never mind," Lita said, bringing her beverage to her

lips. "This cafeteria is most excellent. The view of the city is just gorgeous. Thank you for bringing us here Leo."

"Look at that beautiful sunset," Vicki said, nodding in agreement. "I have not seen such beautiful sun colors reflecting on the clouds, ever. And the little fishing boats are so cute. What are they fishing in November?"

"Fish!" I remarked with a cheeky laugh. "They are connected with a rope. You can tell that there are in small groups of five or six boats by their little boat lights' arrangement."

"So, how did your uncle's funeral go?" Lita asked me, changing the subject, plucking a cigarette out of a Marlborough pack with her lips. She turned the box toward me.

"Thank you, I don't smoke," I said. "The funeral went well by all accounts, I thought. Thank you for asking. Somehow, I thought you were not aware of what was going on."

"That's not nice. I paid attention. I just did not want to make a big deal out of it. Were you close with your uncle?"

I was surprised by her question. I did not think she would care to know.

"Yes, I was. He was very much a father figure for me. It feels weird somehow. In past discussions with him he thought he would never die, which, of course, made no sense."

"Oh! Do I see a lonely, sad face and eyes ready to get teary?" Lita asked, bringing her face closer to mine.

"Leo, are you are sad?" Nancy added.

Vicki got interested. She rearranged her body in her chair to take a good look at me. I wiped away the two tears that found the courage to drop down my cheeks. This was the first time since Patra where my uncle died that I felt his loss, in front of these three women that I hardly knew. The women rose and surrounded my chair. One by one, they went down on their knees before comforting me within their group hug. I had a glimpse of Eleni behind the bar. She looked astonished at the scene she was watching: a teary man seated on a chair with three American women on their knees hugging and caressing him.

The group hug lasted a few minutes. Vicki and Nancy were the first to return to their seats. Lita stayed a few seconds longer holding me. I let my fingers rest on her head, slightly brushing her blonde hair back and forth before finally prompting her to stand up.

"That was emotional," she said, taking a deep breath and looking straight into my wet eyes, as she sat in her chair. "And sexy!"

Nancy lit a cigarette. "Come on Lita. Give him a break. What do you do for a living, Leo?" she posed the question exhaling smoke at the same time. I interpreted the question as an attempt to divert my emotions.

"I am a Vice Principal in an Adult Education Centre in Vancouver. Before that, I was a teacher teaching Math and Physics."

"Math and Physics? Wow! I hate both subjects," Nancy grunted. "Vicki and Lita like math. They are studying to become engineers. I am on languages."

"Really? You study engineering?" I said, turning toward the other two women and wiping the corner of my eyes with my two thumbs.

"Yes, my dear," Lita said. "Please wipe the surprised look off your face. Vicki and I are in our second years in UCLA's engineering program. Nancy is studying to become a secondary teacher, teaching Spanish and French. We are not just good looking; we are also smart."

"You could certainly be," I said, standing up still smiling. "I couldn't tell this listening to you screaming 'more' in the middle of the night. Please excuse me. I need to use the boys' room."

"Oh stop that!" Lita countered. "I see you are back to your normal self again. Making jokes. Like you did not wish you were the one doing ME!"

Vicki and Nancy giggled. I laughed as well, giving Lita two thumbs up before turning to walk back toward the bar.

I asked Eleni where the washrooms were. She asked me if I was okay. I said I was. But she did not seem to believe my answer. With hesitation, she pointed out that the washrooms were to the left of the entrance doors. Then, politely and with a hint of humor, she asked me if I needed help with concluding my washroom business. I kindly refused her offer while checking why my phone was vibrating. It was a text from Troy asking where I was, and that she missed me. I mentioned this to Eleni.

"Don't tell her you are here with me and the Americans. She would go crazy, Leo," she murmured.

I thought about it for a few seconds. Then on my way to the washroom I texted the following: "Hi Troy. My phone is dying. I am at Kastraki having a drink. I will see you soon. All is OK."

Coming back to the bar, I saw the Americans in the balcony romancing the view. The small blue lights at the bottom edge of the aluminum rail were highlighting their naked legs. Their silhouetted bodies, supported by their hands holding the rail, were slightly bent forward. I stepped out onto the balcony. It took me a few seconds to appreciate in the quilt of the settling night, the back view of their three bodies side by side. Lita turned around.

"Are you enjoying the view Leo?" she asked with a huge grin on her face.

"Yes. Very much so," I said with a smile. "Please do not

mind me. Feel free to watch the view."

She laughed. Nancy and Vicki turned sideways.

"Hm! He is not sad any longer. And I think he does not like our front view," Nancy mocked me. She turned her back on me and rested her upper body against the rail, prominently offering me the view of her buttocks and slightly open legs. "Is this view better?" she asked, looking toward the thousands of city lights cracking the darkness at the far end of the Messinian gulf.

"Both views are excellent," I said, joining them by the rail. I held Nancy's hand and raised it along with mine, pointing toward the city lights. "But this view… I am in love with."

"You are such a teaser," Lita said, nudging my shoulder.

"But he is romantic," Nancy replied, unlocking her hand to caress my cheek. "I love him already."

"Can we go inside?" Vicki interrupted. "It's getting chilly."

Inside we went and we ordered more drinks from the male server who approached our table. Eleni's shift was over and she made the point of coming by our table and kissing me goodnight before leaving. The Americans did not look happy that she did not say goodnight to them. They criticized the way her sexy body moved through the tables and eventually disappeared behind the entrance doors. As far as I was concerned, they were jealous. For the next hour or so, the talk was about what men want from women and vice versa. When finally we left the premises and said our goodnights in the parking lot, I agreed to meet them at noon, for lunch, at Electra's roof top cafeteria.

When I arrived at Auntie's apartment at around 10 o'clock, Auntie, Mom, and Troy were having a snack on the balcony, listening to some sort of a concert taking place at the park. Of course, I had to tell them where I was and what I did during the time I was gone. Troy listened to me, quite relaxed, and she did not seem to care at all that I was with the Americans. Mom was almost upset with the idea that I was with Lita, reminding me about the horrible night she had to endure in Apollon hotel, in Patra.

Auntie cautioned me to be careful with women I did not know. She carefully stated that only Greek women like Troy are women of truth and trust and willing to stand by their man. Therefore, I should not be looking far away from the tree, if there was a need for me to fill the void of a failed marriage. And there, with loud music tantalizing the soft November's night air, we all engaged into a conversation about what constitutes a failing marriage, how a true marriage should be, and what encompasses infinite and passionate love, aka *latria*.

The Trip to Trachila

Mom and Auntie decided to go to Trachila, Mom's village, for a day. I agreed to drive them, fully aware that I was reneging on my promise to meet the Americans for lunch. Somehow I knew that I would not see them again. But I was okay with that though. Troy was to accompany us until Kastania, Auntie's village, where we were going to drop off *Papou* Panagiotis.

I loved going to Trachila ever since I was a child. This traditional, beautiful fishing village in Western Mani is located at the end of a snaky mountainous road, 55 kilometers to the southeast of Kalamata. It is named after the shape of the nearby cape that looks like a *trachillos* aka neck. Many of the houses built at the bottom of the mountain and literally on top of rocks, allow residents to observe the crystal clear waters in the summer near and far. But in the winter, the waves cause havoc as they break on the rough rocks and allow the wind to raise the water droplets high enough to whip the buildings without mercy.

My fond memories of Trachila include the festivals called *panigiri*: the burning of the effigy of Judas on the day of Easter; the day of Saint John on June 23rd of every year; and the village fair in September. During those days it was a guarantee that all of our relatives would return to Trachila from other parts of Greece and sometimes abroad. Many other visitors, Greeks or tourists, would also populate the small square outside the small Byzantine old church of St. John's on the night of the festivities.

Festival goers would eat, drink, and dance to the melodies of the live band. Gypsies would circulate amongst the participants selling children's toys and balloons. When there wasn't enough room for everyone to get a chair and a table by the church's square, more tables would be set up on the cemented flat terrain by the harbor, located directly underneath the square. The festivities would continue until late into the night. Us children were allowed to stay up late: playing in the harbor's promenade or around the village's small streets lit by many strings of colorful light bulbs. The day after was a cleaning and quiet day as the village would resolve back in its normal activities.

It did not take me long to remember how to get to Kastania—Greek translation is chestnut—a village occupying the eastern side of Taygetos mountain in Mani. I asked Auntie if anything had changed in the village since I was there last, almost ten years ago. She answered, "Everything is the same since I was a child. Nothing changed." Papou Panagiotis seconded that before starting his WWII story in the mountains of Epirus.

"I remember when Metaxas, the Prime Minister, said 'NO' to Mussolini," he sighed. "Most men in Kastania went to Kalamata to join the army. We wanted to fight the Italian

Fascists who invaded our country on 28 of October, in 1940. They put us on a train to Athens and then on a train to Thessaloniki to a training facility. What training? After one week they sent us in Epirus. It was already January, 1941."

"Epirus?" I asked.

"Yes. Damn Epirus… so rugged and mountainous. And we were in Southern Albania. It was so cold that we had to sleep as close to each other as possible, to generate some heat. We were wearing many layers of clothing; the lucky ones had long coats. And we were full of fleas."

"Fleas? In the freezing cold?" Troy sounded scared.

"Damn fleas. They live everywhere," Papou added.

"My boots had holes and the snow would get inside and melt, freezing my toes. Luckily, I found a dead Italian who had my shoe size so I took his boots. That's why we killed the Italians. So, we could take their clothes. They would watch us from far away doing this and they thought we were eating the dead bodies."

"I think this war is known as the Greco-Italian war," I said. "In the beginning, the Italians came from Albany, then a protectorate of Italy, and advanced to the Greek border where they met the Greek army. But then the Greek army pushed them back."

"Yes, that happened in March," said Papou. "I remember our Captain told us that he had orders for our unit to attack. We freaked out. We could see the Italian fires across the ridge and their canons reflecting the moon's bright light. We were cold, hungry, and many of us had no bullets. One soldier mentioned that to the Captain. 'Perhaps we should wait for the morning for re-enforcements Captain,' another soldier said. The Captain stood up, secured the knife to the top of his gun, and pointed across the ridge to the direction of the enemy. 'There is warmth and food over there,' he said.

'I am hungry. Let's go shopping in the Italian market and get something to eat.'

"So, we all stood up and attacked under the moonlight's guidance screaming 'AERA ρε κερατάδες' (AIR you bastards). The Italians heard the screaming and the echo in the cold night was tremendous. They got so scared that they did not fire a single bullet. They left everything they had and ran. We took the ridge and secured the area, but instead of celebrating our Captain organized us so that we all had a warm Italian meal. That was the best food I ever had. In the morning we arrested many Italians who were hidden all over the mountain."

"I think it was in April, 1941 when the Germans made a detour from going to Russia and attacked Greece," I pointed out. "That was Operation Marita."

"True," Papou Panagiotis added. "You know your history. In April, we heard that the Germans were coming from Bulgaria and they were behind our lines. We knew we were outnumbered and outgunned. Metaxas surrendered the country to Germans and the Italians. Me and a couple of other guys decided to leave Albania on our own without telling our officers. We were scared that although the Germans said they would let us return to our homes they were going to kill us.

"It took me almost a month and a half to reach Kalamata, and then Kastania. Most of my travel was by foot. But I had a lot of help from other co-patriots along the way. They would feed me and give me clothes and shoes and a place to sleep. At times, I would get a donkey ride from a village to the next. I remember when I reached Kastania I went down to my knees, kissed the ground, and started to cry like a child."

"You are lucky to be alive," Auntie said. Everyone

agreed. I added some historical facts to the story.

"Hitler blamed the failure of his invasion of the Soviet Union, which had to be delayed, on Mussolini's failed conquest of Greece. Some say that it was just an excuse that Hitler used to deflect blame from himself to his ally, Italy, but we Greeks agreed with Hitler."

"Can we talk about something else?" Troy begged. "Do we have to talk about WWII?"

We did change the subject and talked about the political climate in Greece all the way to Kastania. As I drove through the last part of the narrow road climbing the mountain to the top of the plateau that runs from the *Kalyves* (old houses) to *Pyrgos* (castle), I recalled that the village in its earlier days was very important in the area. And not by accident, I thought, as across the mountains one can find Byzantine Mistras. In addition, the village, invisible from the coast, tucked into a low valley and under the lower slopes of the Taygetos Mountain, offered a strategic advantage point to the Greeks against enemies.

I parked the car in the central square. There were a couple of senior citizens having coffee in the village's only coffee shop. Papou Panagiotis joined them. He shook hands with them and addressed them by name. Mom, Troy, and Auntie went into St. John's church—a few meters away from the coffee shop, and lit a candle. I waited patiently by the car for them to come back. Then, leaving Papou behind to enjoy his coffee and his friends, we took a steep, uphill, narrow street – rocky, precipitous and labyrinthine it was. It led to Auntie's patriarchal house made from mountain rocks glued together with white-painted cement.

Auntie opened the door, using a black, old-fashioned key. There was an old clothing smell in the air. She opened all the windows on her way to the kitchen. I dropped the two small suitcases I was carrying by the couch. Mom followed her into the kitchen while Troy opened the doors to the balcony. You could smell the mountain in the fresh November air storming inside the room and filling every space.

"We will rest," Auntie said. "Then we will leave for Trachila."

Troy went to the coffee shop and came back with cold beverages and some snacks. We all indulged, having them on the balcony. Too bad, I thought, it was not summer so that I could hear the noise that Greek crickets—called γρύλος (Grilos) in Greek or *tzitziki*, make. And that noise, apparently, comes from flapping their wings very fast to keep them cool. I remembered my favorite game as a child: running without shoes in a plain dry field and watch the crickets jump all over between and around my feet to the left and to the right. Hundreds and hundreds of them! Uncle George was excellent at spotting them on the trees, interestingly enough, as the insects are great in camouflaging themselves.

An hour later, I was driving down the mountain, toward the connector to the main road leading to Trachila. Auntie was quiet but Mom was chatty. She started telling a story about when her family escaped the wrath of the Greek communists during the civil war that shook up Greece following WWII. She told us how one of her cousins survived a killing spree.

"The communists would kill the villagers who stood against them," she said. "Then they would throw the dead bodies down the village's well, so that nobody could use the water again. The bullet just scratched Stelios' head and they thought he was dead, you see, because the blood was running down his face. They threw him down the well on top of the other bodies. As new bodies kept falling down the well, he would slowly and carefully move his body to the wall of the well, keeping cover under two or three bodies."

"That's amazing," I murmured. "Pure luck."

"Luck?" Mom said. "At the end, one of the killers called from the top of the well to see if anyone was still alive. 'Tell me if you are alive and I will save you,' the communist said. Stelios did not move or say anything but across the well someone moaned. The communists poured gasoline down the well and set the bodies on fire. Because Stelios was two or three levels below dead people he escaped the fire that was consuming the top bodies. Then after a few hours he was able to climb out of the well gasping for air. That's better than luck."

I agreed. If it's not someone's time to die it will not happen no matter what. Uncle had escaped death a few times according to him. I told Mom and Auntie the story he told me, when the 'bucket' he was sailing with was caught in a major storm and the engines died. The ship with no power was hermetically engulfed by the huge waves. Everyone was praying to Jesus and all the Saints to save them. Only Uncle kept trying to fix the engine with a flashlight in his mouth, often falling down as the ship was violently pushed in all directions by the waves. And finally, he was successful in starting the emergency battery and, soon after, the main engines all by himself.

"Jesus and the Saints will not help you if you don't do something yourself," I said. "That's what Uncle told me."

"My George," Auntie said with a sigh. "He never gave up. He saved so many lives."

We reached the small picturesque port and beach of Agios Nikolaos. The November sunrays, although not very warm, were bright enough, highlighting the amazing beach with its thousands of large rocks. Packed randomly, they allowed the dark seawater to smoothly enter between them and then withdraw at its own convenience.

We passed one of the most beautiful coasts of the area, the beach of Pantazis, which has gray sand and gorgeous turquoise waters. Then, soon after that, I could see the small island of Pefnos where the beautiful Helen of Greece was born. Of course, after Paris's elopement with her, she became Helen of Troy; and hence, this was one of the immediate causes of the Trojan War. Paris was the son of King Priam and Queen Hecuba of Troy.

I asked Mom and Auntie if they wanted to stop to take a look at the stalagmites in the cave Katafygi that was coming up. They refused. I did not blame them. It was getting late in the afternoon and they had probably seen the cave many times before. So, I kept following the snaky road of Agios Dimitrios along the coast. The road was narrow with cliffs dropping down to the sea on one side and cacti and bushes supporting the man-cut mountainside on the other.

"Do you see the cape?" Mom said, pointing to the cape appearing at the far end of the road. "That's where I and the other young girls from Trachila would take our goats."

"Really?" I said. "Did your goat have a name?"

Mom looked puzzled. "*Katsiki*," she grunted. "Her name was *katsiki*."

"Hm! *Katsiki* means goat. You mean you named your goat, goat? You did not name her like we name dogs?"

"No. Her name was *katsiki*. All the girls' goats had the name *katsiki*. We just differentiated them using our last names. Mine was Thimouleas' katsiki."

"My George told me that one time he had to save the goat from the German bullets," Auntie interrupted.

"Yes," Mom answered. "We were in Kalamata that dark and miserable from the rain night. The Greek soldiers were attacking the Germans who were defending the Mylos. My dad locked us in the house and snuffed out all the candles. But he forgot the *katsiki* tied on a rope in the courtyard. My mom started screaming, 'Oh my God. Where is the *katsiki*, Yanni? You left the *katsiki* out? The Germans will kill it.' My dad was too scared to go out and get the animal but our George was brave. He took a knife and went out. With bullets flying all around him he cut the rope and got the *katsiki* safe into the house with us. We were so happy to see him and the animal. We hugged them and kissed them in the dark for a few minutes. But then we had to give milk to the goat to keep it quiet as it kept bleating and bleating. I guess the poor thing was in distress or hungry or whatever."

We reached the outskirts of Trachila. All of the sudden the road diminished to a one car-length pavement. I maneuvered through it to reach the small church of Agios Yannis (St. John). I continued driving with extreme caution along the paved street build on top of the rocks. There were four older women seated by a table in the 'Kafenion Trachila'. A couple of cats asleep under the table were not bothered by the small dog walking nearby.

"This is Maria," Mom shouted. "Stop the car. This is my cousin."

I stopped the car and we all tumbled out. Mom's cousin screamed from excitement. They hugged and kissed. Then Auntie followed with her own hugs and kisses. And then it was my turn to get hugged and kissed. We were introduced to the other women. One of them, she looked like she was over one hundred years old, took a long look at me. She held my hands and put her tiny skinny body frame a few millimeters away from mine.

"Panagia mou," she said, allowing me to see her two front teeth – the only ones left in her mouth – as she looked up at my face. "You are Maria's son. Leonarthos! Do you remember me?"

I smiled, feeling uneasy because I could not remember her.

"I used to babysit you and your brother all the time," she continued. "When you guys were swimming there," she pointed to the jetty, down below by the port, "I was seated by the stairs watching you."

"Christa loved you," Mom said laughing. "Don't you remember when she would take you to see the cove? You were so scared when the sea would come thundering in. Don't you remember when you and your brother would fish sea urchins so she could make salad for you guys?"

That last comment rang a bell. I did recall the sea urchin salad, but Uncle making it and not Christa. He would cut the sea urchin in half and drop its inside contents into a soup plate. Then, he would add olive oil and lemon juice, chopped onions, tomatoes and a little parsley, before dipping his *paximathia* (dry bread) in the salad.

"Oh, I remember now," I announced. "Yes, the sea urchin salad."

Christa let my hands go, grabbed the back of my head with both of her hands and pulled it down to her head level. She gave a big kiss to each of my cheeks. And since I was bending my body awkwardly anyway, she followed the kisses with a hug.

"Good Christa," Auntie said. "Last time Leonarthos was here with my George you were in the hospital."

"Our George is gone," Christa said. "You need to take care of yourself now, Eleni mou."

"Yes. You are still young Eleni," Mom's cousin interrupted. "Don't let the grief consume you. You have lost a lot of weight."

"I will be okay," Auntie said. "But we need to go now. We will come and visit later. We just need to go and open the house."

I drove the car to the end of the cement road, where Uncle and Auntie built their two-level summerhouse, just before the start of the dirt road that leads to the cove. A lovely cottage really, overlooking the rest of the village and the open Messinian Gulf. I parked in the designated area and waited for Mom and Auntie who were walking the distance. They arrived shortly. We unloaded the car and rested for a while, before heading back to Kafenion Trachila to meet Mom's cousin and for a bite to eat. It was getting dark and chilly but the beauty of the village settling in its isolation from the rest of the world blanked my mind and allowed me for a moment to dream about nothing.

Vangelis, the owner of the Kafenion Trachila, cooked pork skewers in the grill for us. His wife brought along a Greek salad, two Amstel beers for Mom and I, and a Sprite for Auntie, as she complained of having an upset stomach. Christa and Maria kept us company and soon enough they started telling stories about Uncle George.

Christa told the story about when she and Uncle were kids and they used to play tag. He was rough and he would ignore that she was a girl. He would not only tag her but he would also wrestle her to the ground grunting and beating his chest with his fists rapidly like a gorilla. That was a warning signal to the other kids playing the game to back off or they would be engaged in a battle. And it worked all the time because the other kids were scared to tag him.

Maria, mom's cousin, told us how much she would get teased by Uncle when a man, a few years younger than she was, fell in love with her. In those days it was unacceptable for a woman to be in a relationship with a younger man.

Uncle's tease was that she would die first and he would get a younger woman. However, the most serious issue was Uncle, being her cousin, cared about what other people would think of such a relationship. And Maria stayed single. Not Uncle's fault though. Rather, it was circumstances like her father and mother passing away in a short period of time and taking care of her siblings, which did not allow her time to even think of marriage.

Mom followed with a couple of stories of her own. One was about how my dad met Uncle and another was about the first time Uncle brought Auntie home to introduce her to the family. He talked to Mom and Kaliopi, their other sister, ahead of time, asking them not to judge Auntie as she was a little overweight. He was going to put her on a diet and make her a star. Auntie remembered as well. She was a little overweight at that time. But then she went on a diet herself to make him happy.

I went on to tell my own Uncle George stories as well. One was about him telling me that he knew how to dissolve the pollution cloud hanging over Athens. He would take a helicopter and spray the atmosphere with his invented special aero spray and within a week the pollution would be gone, no longer bothering the Athenians. Another was that one time he was swimming somewhere in Mani and he felt a current coming from the bottom of the sea. He dove downward following the current. To his surprise the water at the point of entry—at the bottom of the sea—did not taste salty but it was regular drinkable water. He figured that an underground stream of natural water coming from the mountain was exiting at the bottom of the sea. He talked to politicians trying to get funding to build an offshore drilling rig to collect the drinkable water. But they laughed at him.

Then, I talked about the time when my young son,

Felitche and I were in Trachila. We had a small inflatable boat that would barely fit two people. Uncle wanted all three of us to be inside the boat and, against my advice he jumped into it, flipping all of us into the water. And speaking of water, he also tried to teach Auntie swimming. His thinking was that if you throw someone in the water, his or her survival instinct would persevere and the person would learn to swim. It worked with me at age four, when he threw me from a boat a few meters away from the beach. I swam, paddling my hands like a dog, all the way back to the shore.

Unfortunately, this did not work with Auntie at age thirty-two. As he threw her off the boat she sank pretty fast, screaming for help. He had to dive after her and save her from drowning. Poor Auntie was so terrified that she would not dare to put her feet in the water when Uncle was nearby. That's when I came into the picture. I was able to gain her trust and with the use of children's arm floats teach her how to swim. Up to this date Auntie uses at least one arm float when she swims.

I did not realize that the women were laughing and crying at the same time listening to my telling. Surely, the night's veil over the village allowing the few lights to discriminate through it was bringing Uncle's spirit back. He was there, somewhere and everywhere, climbing the Trachila rocks and diving into the sea, splashing the water all over. I was at peace!

The Death Paradox Dialogue

In the beginning was the Word, and the Word was
with God, and the Word was God. ~ (John1:1)

Uncle: There is no God. God is a human invention.

Me: It does not matter if you believe in God or not, you
need to consider the concept that there was a beginning.
But, if there was a beginning, then there must be an end.
Such being the case then, everything is driven toward a con-
clusive destruction. My question is twofold: what was before
the beginning and what comes after the destruction?

Uncle: I can tell you that in the beginning there were no
names. Things have no names. We made them up. Every
culture has its own creation story and somehow it starts in a
similar fashion with an Entity or Energy called God or whatever. Why do we have to give it a name?

Me: I believe in the beginning was space and time, not
necessarily in that order, coexisting in multi-dimensional *loop*

points or singularities describing real space-time events, or imaginary ones, or a combination of both. And the *loop* points are relative. That is, they may be interpreted differently depending on the observer's position, for each space-time *loop* point is not necessarily mutually exclusive from other such points that may have different sets of rules and mathematical principles.

Uncle: I don't understand this stuff. What I understand is that in the beginning there was no time because humans were not there to call it time. I don't care about space. Space does nothing for me.

Me: But if you are considering time you must consider space. If you look at this universe and its creation you must see it's beginning as a single point in space-time. That is what scientists call a singularity point—The Big Bang. The theory describes how our universe began—starting from a small singularity and then inflating for the next 14 billion years to the Cosmos we know today. Yet, the most revolutionary concept to me is that time is not a universal measurement. It does not matter how much our lives are governed by rules of nature, the same hours and days and years, time would never be absolute. The rate at which it passes depends entirely on who observes it.

Uncle: Nothing is absolute. Death is not absolute. If there are no observers, then there is no time to record. There is no death. Observers see time going faster or slower. It is meaningless to talk about time. It is meaningless to talk about a beginning and about an end like death. There is no destruction as you put it.

Me: (Grinning) So, you think we will live forever?

Uncle: Wipe that grin off your face. What I am saying is that it does not matter what time it is. We should be looking at the sunrise the same way. Not at what time it happens. I know that the beginning of time is hard to understand. As it is, the end of time is hard to understand. But I don't rush to do things because 'I have no time left'. I don't let time affect my way of living.

Me: Well, time is relative. That is a fact. It has been shown in many experiments that the rate of actual time slows down when particles like photons speed up. In Einstein's theory of relativity, time dilation describes the difference of elapsed time between two events. That is, the faster we go, the more the time is affected. If you travel in space with the speed of light, you actually don't grow older at the same rate as people on Earth do.

Uncle: Whatever Einstein said. Of course, the white-haired man had nothing to do but watch time go by. My question is simple. When I die, is time over for me or still running?

Me: It is still running for time is infinite. But obviously not for you; you are dead. It runs for me because I am alive. We were holding two observer points. But now that you are dead you are no longer an observer. You do not exist.

Uncle: Oh, I see. I was holding an observer's point and now that I am dead I cease to observe. But who knows if I am still observing or not? Because I am not breathing, it does not mean I am not part of time. Or another time!

Me: Uncle, you are dead. You no longer influence time. But your death, that precise point, will influence time for, at least, this universe. No matter how infinitesimally small that influence may be. There would still be a 'wrinkle' in time due to your death.

Uncle: But, how do you see or perceive things only in one direction and not in another? How do you know that I am dead? Perhaps I am not. What if I am watching you from behind a hologram, and perhaps I can still influence your real time or whatever you perceive to be real from my 'another' time.

Me: (Laughing) Like a ghost? Yeah right! Uncle, I would know you are dead, for at least this universe, when your heart stops and your breathing is gone. I am actually getting that mental picture of this happening. It is not difficult to understand. Our time starts when we are conceived—and this is another topic for discussion as some people may argue that we are not fully human when we are conceived; and our time ends when we die. The reason why there is time is because of our human connection with time. There is a perception and different understanding of how time passes and how it drags; but we grow and change and we get the chance to do something with our time as it flows and messes up our senses. Now, I can accept the question: Is Death the End of Time?

Uncle: That's a good question, isn't it? And I will make it more complex. Is Death the End or Real Time or Imaginary Time—what I called 'another' time, or both? Because I bet, your 'multi-dimensional space-time *loop* points' are somehow mapped on real and imaginary axes. Correct?

Me: Yes. Time can be real or imaginary. But space cannot be imaginary. Can it?

Uncle: I told you I don't care about space. Here is my problem. I cannot accept that Death is the end of time for the person who is dead. And I don't invite ideas about heaven and hell and all that religious stuff. I am saying that, in reality, there is no such thing as time by itself. For if you have a beginning of time then there is a problem as you must have an end of time. But Time has no beginning or an end? It is just a label. So, if there is no time to record, then there is no death to record either. Death is a label.

Me: I don't disagree with your thinking of the concept we

call time. For me it is still difficult to ignore how things have happened in the past and how they are working in the present. I like to live in the present moment as much as possible and I want to be able to influence how things would work in the future. And for me, Death is real, no matter how much of a philosophical spin you want to give to the concept. For I have killed an animal and eaten the animal I killed.

Uncle: (Laughing) I will tell you part of the future. Our sun is less than halfway through its life span. There would not be humans watching that wonderful death a few billion years from now. Even if Earth is not destroyed by then, from us humans, the creatures living on Earth would not be humans.

Me: Well, we both are not going to be alive then to see if you are right, Uncle.

Uncle: You are absolutely right. We would be on another universe on another timeline or perhaps on another hologram.

Episode 12

The Resurrection

The flight back to Vancouver from Athens and through Amsterdam was a pleasant one. I felt a little bit under the weather but mainly, I was happy when the plane touched down in Richmond, BC. My brother, Yannis, came to pick up Mom and I. He filled me in with what was going on with my family and I told him how things went in Greece. Mom kept quiet. We first took Mom to my sister's house in Burnaby and then my brother drove me to Coquitlam, dropping me off in the cul-de-sac, in front of my house.

Felitche, my oldest son, came running down the driveway and jumped into my arms full of joy to see me again. Clarice, my wife, although she looked happy to see me did not refuse the opportunity to make silly remarks.

"Did you enjoy your time in Greece Leo?" she joked.

"Yes I did! Especially my uncle's funeral."

"Well, at least you did not have to take care of the kids for two weeks."

"No I did not."

"Did you see your old girlfriends? Did they make you happy?"

I did not answer back. I was just happy to see my family again.

A week later, Clarice gave me a letter that had arrived from Athens, Greece. It was addressed to me but she had opened it.

"It is from your girlfriend," she announced with a sneaky smile. "She missed you already. I wish I could read Greek."

I did not find her action appropriate and I was angry. However, I decided not to engage in a conversation. I drew the letter out of the envelope. It was from Troy.

THE LETTER FROM TROY

My love!

Do I have the right to call you 'my love?' I think I do, because no matter how you feel about me, the fact is that I love you. Hence, you are my love. And you will remain my love, aside from what the future is hiding from us.

When we were kids I had that DREAM to be with you, to hold you and kiss you every morning and every night. And then, life took you away and at age sixteen I was married to a husband I did not want. And then, a few days ago, we kissed. And everything started to burn inside me until my heart exploded from passion and love. I stopped fighting to forget you. I refused to let you go. I decided to surrender to me loving you and give up my freedom to think sensibly.

Please forgive me if what I am saying sounds crazy. I KNOW it's crazy. I know it makes no sense. I know I will not have you. Or will I? Should I? Is life going to give me a present or a miracle perhaps? I want to believe that somehow, someday, we will be together but my heart cries as I know you will forfeit me. You will abandon me like the lonely streams that run through the dessert are abandoned by the rain to their demise.

Can you hear my cry? Can you feel my breath surrounding my tears? They make my eyes puffy and sore, my tears. They keep falling. I see a flower and I see you. I see the sky and I see you. I see the sea and I see you. I see the world and I see you. I would die for you. Would you believe that? The infinite and absolute surrender of my world for you becomes beautiful like the myriads of worlds and stars in the universe. I will search a thousand lives to find you. To hold you and kiss you! To make you mine again and again and again!

I ask myself, what makes me happy? The answer is: 'YOU DO!'

Who is the most important person in my life? The answer is: 'YOU ARE!'

I took a week off from work. I cannot stop thinking of you. I cannot concentrate. I think I will go to a pharmacist to get anti-depressants (I see you laughing but it's not funny!). My head is hurting and I can feel every beat of my heart. What should I do? Whom should I tell? Will you reply to my letter? No, wait. Please don't, if your letter is going to hurt me more than I am hurting now.

I would love you forever!
YOUR Troy xoxoxox

THE RESPONSE TO TROY

Hi Eleni,

Thank you for your letter. I think I understand your feelings. Yet, there is only one sentence that describes my feelings toward you: I love you as a friend and as a sister.

I know that probably this is not what you wanted to hear, but for me, to be in a relationship other than the one that includes my family would be detrimental to everyone around me.

I am thinking that I could probably write things to you to trigger false expectations; to make you happy and hopeful. But that would not be fair and I have too much respect for you to do such a thing. I cannot ask you to forgive me when I tell you that my family is my first and most important thing to my life right now, because it's nothing to forgive. IT JUST IS!

I care deeply for you. So, what can I do to help you? I don't know. Your love toward me, I feel, is extraordinary. My love toward you is important—if I dare to point that out. For you are a part of my thoughts and my history. But you are not MY LOVE the same way you are describing I am YOUR LOVE.

I wish you the best! Until next time we meet, take care,
Leonarthos

A few days after I sent the letter, I was visiting Mom when Auntie called her on the phone to see how we were doing. I talked to Auntie briefly. She said Stefano phoned her asking for me. I told her to relay to him that I could not find his cousin Michali. Finally, Troy told her everything. Auntie's suggestion to her was to forget me and to proceed with her life. Troy got upset but agreed. Apparently, all was good now and everyone in Greece was preparing for the Christmas holidays three weeks away.

I couldn't wait for Christmas. Although going back to my job with the Vancouver School Board as Acting Principal of Roberts Education Centre made me forget the crazy trip in Greece, it also built my anxiety and stress to maximum levels. I found things around the Centre a step behind where they were supposed to be. The teachers' schedules were not organized for the February semester, and the Centre was not set up for closing over the holidays. And at home, Clarice was stressing me out with her usual Christmas shopping, mostly useless gifts, resulting in maximizing my credit cards.

I woke up with a headache the Sunday morning of the first weekend after the closing of schools for the holidays. I sat quietly in the kitchen drinking the coffee that Clarice had prepared, thinking that I would not accept Lita's Facebook friendship invitation. Clarice interrupted my thoughts.

"It is 10:30 and the kids are still asleep," she said. "It is raining a storm outside. You had a nightmare last night. You were screaming in your sleep. Do you remember your dream?"

"Vividly… I think I saw my uncle. He was in the bow of a cargo ship battling the rough seas. He was wearing a yellow raincoat and brown gumboots. He was holding a pole and laughing as the ship's bow was going in and out of the waves which smashed him at every opportunity they got. He saw me screaming from the bridge to get out of harm's way. But he kept laughing. Then, all of the sudden, he was standing by my side on the bridge; and all went quiet. 'Get the olive tree,' he said.

"What olive tree?"

"I have no idea. I woke up."

"Probably that was the time when I pushed you to try and wake you up. Are you going to get the Christmas lights? The kids want to decorate the outside of the house today. Rona's has a sale."

Rona's Home Store in Coquitlam was full of customers but I knew what I was looking for and it did not take me long to get a few packs of strings of lights.

"Is that all?" the young teller behind the counter asked after I put the lights on top of it.

"Yes," I said, avoiding looking at her but rather letting my eyesight follow a customer's shadow going out of the store through the two large automatic doors. The teller scanned the merchandise codes.

"$82.45, please."

I ignored her.

"Are these plants outside for sale?" I asked, nodding in the direction of the parking lot.

"Yes they are," she responded, like she knew what I was talking about.

"I shall be right back," I said. "Please keep my stuff available behind the counter. You may continue with other customers. I shall be right back."

I could feel her eyes checking me out and expressing frustration as I walked outside the store. But I had spotted something that triggered my curiosity and needed an immediate examination.

"Hi there," I said to the small tree bending my knees and kneeling down on the wet cement. The raindrops doing jumping jacks on top of the temporary roof cover, built to protect the small trees and other plants grew erratic and loud. "What are you doing here in the middle of the winter?"

"It's an olive tree, isn't it?"

I looked up. The old man's hat covered most of his head allowing me to view his smile but not his eyes as he was looking down on me and the tree. His yellow raincoat covered his body all the way down to his brown gumboots.

"Yes it is." I said looking back at the tree. "It's a small olive tree. I have not seen anything like it, ever, here in Canada."

"It does not look healthy," he remarked. "The winters here are too cold for such Mediterranean trees. I think this one is already dead."

"You may be right," I grunted. "I think it needed a bigger pot, protection from the cold, and some better care." I touched the thin leaves. A few fell off.

"Well, the price is right for a dead olive tree," his words came from a distance. "Although, I wouldn't pay anything for it."

I stood up to see him slowly moving away, his back facing me. His right index finger pointed at the dark clouds above.

"ONLY $10.99 WITH A 50 PERCENT OFF," he shouted!

Where did he see the price? I wondered. There was no price label on the tree or the pot. Nevertheless, I went back to the store carrying the pot like a baby, to pay for all of my merchandise.

Back in the house, I carefully transferred the baby olive tree into a bigger pot. I added some extra soil and fertilizer. I moved the pot in the covered area of the balcony to protect the tree from the harsh weather but still allow it to get used to it. Clarice and Felitche came to see what I was doing.

"How much did it cost you?" Clarice asked.

"It was about $6 dollars. 50 percent of $10.99, plus tax," I replied.

"It is dead Leo. Why did you get it?"

"We shall see," I murmured. "Perhaps you are right. In any case, it would be protected in this area of the balcony. It may come back. I plan to cover it with a blanket to save it from freezing."

"Why don't you bring it inside the house, Daddy?" Felitche asked touching the leaves.

"Be careful, Felitche," I said calmly, holding his hand and moving it away from the tree, as more leaves fell down. "It is very delicate and it is a little bit sick. Olive trees are outside trees. I worry that if I bring it in, the leaves may die faster because of the dryness of the air inside the house. And then the rest of the tree may also die."

"Should we give it a name?" Felitche asked again.

"Yes! We shall call it…. George. Uncle George."

Later on in the spring, I moved a happy Uncle George to the front of the yard so it could enjoy the warmer sunrays. The last frost was gone and the leaves were rejuvenated having a wonderful dark green color, unique only to the olive trees. And soon after, a few tiny green baby olives spit out to say hello to the world.

UNCLE GEORGE WAS RESURRECTED!

About Leonardo Hutchinson

Leonardo (Leo) Hutchinson was born and raised in Greece. He immigrated to Canada in 1979 at the age of nineteen. He graduated from UBC as a Math and Physics teacher in 1989. In 1997, he completed his Masters' in Education and eventually became a Principal in Vancouver School Board's Adult education system.

His students and colleagues knew him as a gifted teacher who managed to balance excellent organization and discipline with unflagging creativity and spontaneity. He was enthusiastic, compassionate, supportive and inspiring. Students in an adult education system offer a wide range of abilities, educational backgrounds, and language proficiency. Leo embraced these challenges, finding the demands of the classroom as well as the demands of an administrator in adult education engaging rather than daunting. He has written curriculum for classroom and/or self-paced courses for a wide variety of subjects and many of his short stories were shared amongst students in one of his initiatives to enhance literacy.

Beyond his work with staff and students, Leo developed new programs, re-wrote outdated ones and search endlessly for new and exciting resources to infuse into the classroom. He served on various committees and associations over the years and he presented on many professional development days: from instructing teachers on how to work with adult students who have learning disabilities, to showing how to teach Math upgrading courses to ESL students.

While doing his PhD, Leo decided to compile and

publish a few of his short stories. *The Death and Resurrection of Uncle George* is creative non-fiction writing, demonstrating a Greek cultural background that tolerates death as part of life. The book does not have chapters; rather it has episodes that take the reader into different parts of the story with a continuous flow. Yet, short stories are embedded between episodes providing a connection with the past. A metaphor of 'resurrecting Uncle George' proposes that death may not be the end of life.

Made in the USA
San Bernardino, CA
13 January 2019